How to Get Rid of "it"

Before "it" Gets Rid of You

Topical Handbook for
Healing and Deliverance
from Tormenting Emotions

A Practical Self-Help Guide to
Spiritual and Personal Growth

A series of easy spiritual exercises, interactive tools,
And step-by-step instructions to receive
Freedom from bondage
And experience spiritual healing and deliverance

Volume Eight

ISBN-13: 978-1986311762

ISBN-10: 1986311767

How to Get Rid of "it"

Before "it" Gets Rid of You

Topical Handbook for
Healing and Deliverance
from Tormenting Emotions

A Practical Self-Help Guide to
Spiritual and Personal Growth

A series of easy spiritual exercises, interactive tools,
And step-by-step instructions to receive
Freedom from bondage
And experience spiritual healing and deliverance

Volume Eight

Compilations of Works
By
Dr. Paulette Douglas

DEDICATION

**This book is dedicated to my Loving, Supportive, Faithful
Prayer Partners, Instructors, Pastors and Council Friends**

**They have always inspired me to be the Women that God has ordained me to be and to
continue to minister to God's people and to make full proof of my ministry**

CONTENT

How to Get Rid of "it", Before "it" Gets Rid of You

PREFACE

How to Get Rid of "it", Before "it" Gets Rid of You is a Deliverance and Spiritual Warfare Manual compiled by Dr. Paulette Douglas which is worth reading and re-reading more than once, in order to empower the reader when confronting personal crisis and trials. Dr. Paulette Douglas has compiled many practical, spiritual books bringing light to the evil that exists. She brings the deliverance ministry to the forefront, explaining how each and every believer can counteract evil and the devil. Not many believers understand the concept of the Holy Spirit and that we are all called to fight against the devil, our enemy. Dr. Paulette Douglas presents scriptural background and Bible passages from the old and new testaments, as well as prayers to share with the reader that each of us is called to resist and fight against the devil with the power of the Holy Spirit. Dr. Paulette Douglas refers to this as the deliverance ministry and explains this is one of the privileges all believers have at our disposal.

This background scripture material is necessary as many readers may be unfamiliar with these spiritual concepts. The main focus on the book is to be a manual; or one stop guide to show the reader what the bible has to say about deliverance as well as to expose the works and deceptions of the devil as well. The cover itself might seem an actual handbook- yet this book is truly a manual for deliverance. This exhaustive book contains too much information to be digested in a single, quick reading. The words contained are life changing. While some traditional readers and those in organized religion may find this book difficult to believe and a bit theatrical, a close-minded attitude is exactly what the devil wants in order to operate.

It is important to keep in mind the charismatic background of Dr. Paulette Douglas is based on the belief of the real workings of the Holy Spirit and the literal belief in modern day spiritual gifts such as tongues and healing. Much of the book is an invaluable resource where Dr. Douglas has taken scriptural truths and prayers and relates them to the modern-day believer to use and apply when facing any trial or work from the enemy. The scriptural references will empower any reader with a quick resource of how to respond in faith to any difficulty- large and small. It is a spiritual self-help book in the fact that it will allow the reader the tools to look within himself/her-self and identify any areas or issues where Satan has his foothold. Not only that it tells the reader how to face and address these issues! For those who are at a loss of how to begin to approach their spiritual problems there are a number of sample prayers applicable to any number of situations. The reader will get the impression as if this book was written for his or her own situation. This is a book to meditate on and use- and is not intended to collect dust on a book shelf. There are eleven sequels to this handbook which address many other issues that just might cover your "it".

In this twelve-book series, How to Get Rid of "it" Before "it" gets Rid of You we discuss evil spirits and how they operate:
1. The Apostolic anointing and ministry
2. How demons enter and oppress people
3. Curses and how to deal with them
4. Breaking bondages

5. Casting out spirits
6. Healing the wounded heart
7. Ungodly beliefs
8. Ministering to people
9. House cleansing
10. Discerning of spirits

In this volume we deal with the root causes of the "it' of tormenting emotions and How to get rid of the "it" of the tormenting emotions before it gets rid of you. Tormenting emotions is something what plagues many people today, whether tormenting emotions to conquering additions such as food, sex, drugs, alcohol, smoking, spending, masturbation, porn, etc. Some inexperienced deliverance ministers might go after a spirit of the tormenting emotions, which may bring freedom, but often, it doesn't bring lasting freedom. Many times, there is a root that needs to be pulled up, alongside casting out any residing spirits that are holding the person in bondage to the tormenting emotions. Getting to the root of the tormenting emotions is the key to bringing a person lasting genuine freedom. I am going to address the most common roots to tormenting emotions, and hopefully give you an idea of how this bondage works so that you can minister lasting freedom to this type of bondage.

"It Is Finished"
The Words of Victory

"When Jesus therefore had received the vinegar, he said, "It is finished.""—John 19:30
Words of triumph. In His words, "My God, my God, why hast thou forsaken me?" we heard the Savior's cry of desolation. In His words, "I thirst" we listened to His cry of lamentation. Now there falls upon our ears His cry of jubilation— "It is finished." From the words of the victim we turn now to the words of the Victor. The Cross of Christ has two great sides to it: it showed the profound depths of His humiliation, but it also marked the goal of the Incarnation, and further, it told the consummation of His mission, and it forms the basis of our salvation.

It is finished." What is found in these three words, "It is finished" is wrapped up the Gospel of God. In these words, contained the ground of the believer's assurance. In those words, is discovered the sum of all joy, and the very spirit of all divine consolation. Every" it" that we could ever encounter in our lives was dealt with on the cross therefore; we have the victory through Jesus Christ over any and every "it".

"It is finished." This was not the despairing cry of a helpless martyr. It was not an expression of satisfaction that the termination of His sufferings was now reached. It was not the last gasp of a worn-out life. No, rather was it the declaration on the part of the divine Redeemer that all for which He came from heaven to earth to do, was now done; that all that was needed to reveal the full character of God had now been accomplished; that all that was required by the Law before sinners could be saved, had now been performed—that the full price of our redemption was now paid.

"It is finished." The great purpose of God in the history of man was now accomplished—from the beginning, God's purpose has always been one and indivisible. It had been declared to men in numerous ways: in symbol and type, by mysterious hints and by plain intimations, through Messianic prediction and through didactic declaration. That purpose of God may be summarized thus: to display His grace in the creating of children in His own image and glory. And at the Cross the foundation was laid which was to make this possible and actual.

"It is finished." What was finished? The answer to this question is a very full one, though many excellent expositors have sought to limit the scope of these words and to confine them strictly to a single application. We are told it was the prophecies concerning the sufferings of Jesus which were finished, and that He referred only to this. It is readily granted that the immediate reference was to the Messianic predictions, yet we think there are good and sufficient reasons for not confining our Lord's words here to them. Yea, to us it seems certain that Christ referred specially to His sacrificial work, for all Scripture concerning His suffering and shame was not yet fulfilled. There remained the dismissal of His spirit into the hands of the Father (Psa 31:5); there remained the "piercing" with the spear (Zec 12:10: and note that the word used in Psalm 22:16 for the piercing of His hands and feet—the act of crucifixion—is a different one); there still remained the preserving of His bones unbroken (Psa 34:20), and the burial in the rich man's grave (Isa 53:9).

"It is finished." What was finished? We answer His sacrificial work. It is true there yet remained the act of death itself, which was necessary for the making of atonement. But, as is so often the case here in John's Gospel wherein our text is found (cf. Joh 12:23, 31; 13:31; 16:5; 17:4), the Lord here speaks of the completion of His work. Moreover, it must be remembered that the three hours darkness was already past, the awful cup had already been drained, His precious blood had already been shed, the outpoured wrath of God had already been endured; and these are the primary elements in the making of propitiation. The sacrificial work of Jesus, then, was completed, excepting only the act of death which followed immediately. But, as we shall see, the completing of the sacrificial work made an end of several things.

"It is finished."

1. Here we see the accomplished fulfillment of all the prophecies which had been written of Him here He should die. This is the immediate thought of the context: "When Jesus therefore had received the vinegar, He said, It is finished" (John 19:30). Centuries beforehand, the prophets of God had described step by step the humiliation and suffering which the coming Savior should undergo. One by one these had been fulfilled, wonderfully fulfilled, fulfilled to the very letter. Had prophecy declared that He should be the "woman's seed" (Gen 3:15), then He was "born of a woman" (Gal 4:4). Had prophecy announced that His mother should be a "virgin" (Isa 7:14), then was it literally fulfilled (Mat 1:18). Had prophecy revealed that He should be of the seed of Abraham (Gen 22:18), then mark its fulfillment (Mat 1:1). Had prophecy made it known that He

Prophecy said that He should be named before He was born (Isa 49:1), then so it came to pass (Luke 1:30-31). Had prophecy foretold that He should be born in Bethlehem of Judea (Mic 5:2), then mark how this very village was His birthplace. Had prophecy forewarned that His birth should entail sorrowing for others (Jer 31:15), then behold its tragic fulfillment (Mat 2:14-18). Had prophecy foreshown that the Messiah should appear before the scepter of tribal ascendancy had departed from Judah (Gen 49:10), then so He did, for though the ten tribes were in captivity, Judah was still in the land at the time of His advent. Had prophecy referred to the flight into Egypt and the subsequent return into Palestine, (Hose 11:1 and cf. Isa 49:3, 6), then so it came to pass (Mat 2:1415).

Prophecy made mention of one going before Christ to make ready His way (Mal 3:1), then see its fulfillment in the person of John the Baptist. Had prophecy made it known that at the Messiah's appearing "the eyes of the blind shall be opened, and the ears of the deaf shall be unstopped, then shall the lame man leap as a hart, and the tongue of the dumb sing" (Isa 35:56), then read through the four Gospels and see how blessedly this proved true. Had prophecy spoken of Him as "poor and needy" (Psa 40:17, see beginning of Psalm), then behold Him not having where to lay His head. Had prophecy intimated that He should speak in "parables" (Psa 78:2), then such was frequently His method of teaching. Had prophecy depicted Him stilling the tempest (Psa 107:29), then this is exactly what He did. Had prophecy heralded His "triumphal entry" into Jerusalem (Zec 9:9), then so it came to pass!

Prophecy announced that His person should be despised (Isa 53:3), that He should be rejected by the Jews (Isa 8:14), that He should be "hated without a cause" (Psa 69:4), then sad to say, such was precisely the case. Had prophecy painted the whole picture of His degradation and crucifixion, then was it vividly reproduced. There had been the betrayal by a familiar friend, the forsaking by His disciples, the being led to the slaughter, the being taken to judgment, the appearing of false witnesses against Him, the refusal on His part to make defense, the establishing of His innocence, the unjust condemnation, the sentence of capital punishment passed upon Him, the literal piercing of His hands and feet, the being numbered with transgressors, the mockery of the crowd, the casting lots for His garments—all predicted centuries beforehand, and all fulfilled to the very letter. The last prophecy of all which remained here He committed His Spirit into the hands of His Father, had now been fulfilled. He cried "I thirst," and after the tendering of the vinegar and gall, all was now "accomplished"; and as the Lord Jesus reviewed the entire scope of the prophetic Word and saw its full realization, He cried,

"It is finished"!
It only remains for us to point out that as there was a complete set of prophecies which had to do with the first advent of Jesus, so also is there a complete set of prophecies which have to do with His second advent—the latter as definite, as personal, and as comprehensive in their scope as the former. As then we see the actual fulfillment of those which had to do with His first coming to the earth, we may look forward with absolute confidence and assurance to the fulfillment of those which have to do with His second coming. And, as we have seen that the former set of prophecies were fulfilled literally and personally, so also must we expect the latter set to be. To grant the literal fulfillment of the former, and then to seek to spiritualize and symbolize the latter, is not only grossly inconsistent and illogical, but is highly injurious to us and deeply dishonoring to God and to His Word.

"It is finished."
2. Here we see the completion of His sufferings. But what tongue or pen can describe the sufferings of Jesus? The anguish, physical, mental, and spiritual, which He endured! Appropriately was He designated "the man of sorrows": suffering at the hands of men, at the hands of Satan, and at the hands of God. Pain inflicted upon Him by enemies and friends alike. From the beginning He walked the shadows which the Cross cast His path. "I am afflicted and ready to die from my youth up" (Psa 88:15). What a light this throws on His earlier years! Who can say how much is contained in those words? For us, an impenetrable veil is cast over the future; none of us knows what a day may bring forth.

But Jesus knew the end from the beginning! One has only to read through the Gospels to learn how the awful Cross was ever before Him. At the marriage-feast of Cana, where all was gladness and merriment, He makes solemn reference to "his hour" not yet come. When Nicodemus interviewed Him at night, the Savior referred to the "lifting up of the Son of man." When James and John came to request from Him the two places of honor in His coming kingdom, He made mention of the "cup" which He had to drink, and of the "baptism" wherewith He must be baptized. When Peter confessed that He was the Christ, the Son of the living God, He turned to His disciples and began to show unto them "how that he must go unto Jerusalem, and suffer many things of the elders and chief priests and scribes, and be killed, and be raised again the third day" (Mat 16:21). When Moses and Elijah stood with Him on the Mount of Transfiguration, it was to speak of "his decease which he should accomplish at Jerusalem" (Luke 9:31).

If it is true we are quite unable to estimate the sufferings of Christ due to the anticipation of the Cross, still less can we fathom the dread reality itself. The physical sufferings were excruciating, but even this was as nothing compared with His anguish of soul. To a consideration of these sufferings we have already devoted several paragraphs in previous chapters, yet we make no apology in turning to them again. We cannot contemplate too often what Jesus endured to secure our salvation. The better we are acquainted with His sufferings, and the more frequently we meditate thereon, the warmer will be our love and the deeper our gratitude.
At last the closing hours have come. There had been the terrible experience in Gethsemane followed by the appearing before Caiaphas, before Pilate, before Herod, and back again before Pilate. There had been the scourging and mocking by the brutal soldiers; the journey to Calvary; the fastening of His hands and feet to the cruel tree. There had been the reviling of the priests, the crowd, and the two thieves crucified with Him.

There had been the awful cloud that hid from the Father's face, which wrung from Him the bitter cry, "My God, my God, why hast thou forsaken me?" There had been the parched lips which drew from Him the exclamation "I thirst." There had been the fearful conflict with the power of darkness as the serpent "bruised" His heel. But now the suffering is ended. The Lord has bruised Him; man, and Devil have done their worst. The cup has been drained. The awful storm of God's wrath has spent itself. The darkness is ended. The sword of divine justice is done. The wages of sin have been paid. The prophecies of His sufferings are all fulfilled. The Cross has been "endured." Divine holiness has been fully satisfied (Isa 53:11). With a cry of triumph—a loud cry, a cry which reverberated throughout the entire universe—Jesus exclaims, "It is finished." The shame, the suffering and agony, are past. Never again shall He experience pain. Never again shall He endure the contradiction of sinners against Himself. Never again shall He be in the hands of Satan. Never again shall the light of God's countenance be hidden from Him. Blessed be God, all that is finished! "It is finished."

Jesus is concerned in the work of Redemption: He was the One who came here to die for sinners. He is the One who now gives spiritual illumination and understanding, and guides into the truth. Before the Lord Jesus came to this earth, a definite work was committed to Him. In the volume of the book it was written of Him, and He came to do the recorded will of God. Even as a boy of twelve the "Father's business" was before His heart and occupied His attention. Again, in John 5:36 we find Him saying, "But I have greater witness than that of John: for the works which the Father hath given me to finish, the same works that I do." And on the last night before His death, in that wonderful high priestly prayer, we find Him saying, "I have glorified thee on the earth: I have finished the work which thou gavest me to do" (John 17:4).

The mission upon which God had sent His Son into the world was now accomplished. It was not actually finished till He breathed His last, but death was only an instant ahead, and in anticipation of it He cries "It is finished." The demanding work is done. The divinely-given task is performed. A work more honorable and momentous than ever entrusted to man or angels, has been completed. That for which He had left heaven's glory that for which He had taken upon Him the form of a servant, that for which He had remained upon earth for thirty-three years to do, was now consummated. Nothing remained to be added. The goal of the Incarnation is reached. With what joyous triumph must He here have viewed the costly work which, committed to Him, had now been perfected!

"It is finished." The mission upon which God had sent His Son into the world was accomplished. That which had been eternally purposed had come to pass. The plan of God had been fully carried out.

Because He is the Most High, God's will, cannot be thwarted. Because He is supreme, God's counsel must stand. Because He is almighty, God's purpose cannot be overthrown.

"But he is in one mind, and who can turn him? And what his soul desireth, even that he doeth" (Job 23:13). "I know that thou canst do everything, and that no thought can be withholding from thee" (Job 42:2). "But our God is in the heavens: He hath done whatsoever he hath pleased" (Psa 115:3). "There is no wisdom nor understanding nor counsel against the Lord" (Pro 21:30). "For the Lord of hosts hath purposed, and who shall disannul it? And His hand is stretched out, and who shall turn it back?" (Isa 14:27). "Remember the former things of old: for I am God, and there is none else; I am God, and there is none like me: Declaring the end from the beginning, and from ancient times the things that are not yet done, saying, My counsel shall stand, and I will do all my pleasure" (Isa 46:9-10). "And all the inhabitants of the earth are reputed as nothing: and he doeth according to his will in the army of heaven, and among the inhabitants of the earth: and none can stay his hand, or say unto him, What doest thou?" (Dan 4:35). And, in the triumphant cry of the Jesus— "It is finished"—we have a prophecy and pledge of the ultimate carrying out of God's plan completely. At the end of time, when everything is wound up, and God's purpose has been fully consummated, when everything has been done which He before determined should be done, then shall it be said again, "It is finished."

"It is finished."

4. Here we see the accomplishment of the Atonement. Above we have spoken of Christ reaching the goal of the Incarnation, and of the consummation of His mission to the earth; what that goal and mission was, the Scriptures plainly reveal. The Son of Man came here "to seek and to save that which was lost" (Luke 19:10). Christ Jesus came into the world "to save sinners" (1Ti 1:15). God sent forth His Son, born of a woman, "to redeem them that were under the law" (Gal 4:5). He was manifested "to take away our sins" (1Jo 3:5). And all this involved the Cross. The "lost" which He came to seek could only be found there—in the place of death and under the condemnation of God. Sinners could be "saved" only by One taking their place and bearing their iniquities. They who were under the Law could be "redeemed" only by Another fulfilling its requirements and suffering its curse. Our sins could be "taken away" only by their being blotted out by the precious blood of Christ. The demands of justice must be met; the requirements of God's holiness must be satisfied; the awful debt we incurred must be paid. And on the Cross, this was done; done by none less than the Son of God; done perfectly; done once for all.

"It is finished."

That to which so many types looked forward, was now accomplished. A covering from sin and its shame, typified by the coats of skin with which the Lord God clothed our first parents, was now provided. The more excellent sacrifice, typified by Abel's lamb, had now been offered. A shelter from the storm of divine judgment, typified by the Ark of Noah, was now furnished. The only-begotten and well-beloved Son, typified by Abraham's offering up of Isaac, had already been placed upon the altar. A protection from the avenging angel, typified by the shed blood of the Passover-lamb, was now supplied. A cure from the serpent's bite, typified by the serpent of brass upon the pole, was now made ready for sinners. The providing of a life-giving fountain, typified by Moses striking the rock, was now affected.

"It is finished." The Greek word here, teleo, is translated variously in the New Testament. A glance at some of the different renderings in other passages will enable us to discern the fullness and finality of the term used by Jesus. In Matthew 11:1, teleo is rendered as follows, "When Jesus had made an end of commanding his twelve disciples, he departed thence." In Matthew 17:24 it is rendered, "They that received tribute money came to Peter, and said, Doth not your master pay tribute?" In Luke 2:39, it is rendered, "And when they had performed all things according to the Law of the Lord, they returned into Galilee." In Luke 18:31, it is rendered, "All things that are written by the prophets concerning the Son shall be accomplished."

"It is finished." He cried: it is "made an end of"; it is "paid"; it is "performed"; it is "accomplished." What was made an end of? —our sins and their guilt. What was "paid?"—the price of our redemption. What was "performed?"—the utmost requirements of the Law. What was "accomplished?"—the work which the Father had given Him to do. What was "finished?"— the making of atonement. God has furnished at least four proofs that Christ did finish the work which was given Him to do. First, in the rending of the veil, which showed that the way to God was now open. Second, in the raising of Christ from the dead, which evidenced that God had accepted His sacrifice. Third, the exaltation of Christ to His own right hand, which demonstrated the value of Christ's work and the Father's delight in His person. Fourth, the sending to earth of the Holy Spirit to apply the virtues and benefits of Christ's atoning death.

"It is finished." What was "finished?"—the work of atonement. What is the value of that to us? This: to the sinner, it is a message of glad tidings. All that a Holy God requires has been done. Nothing is left for the sinner to add. No works from us are demanded as the price of our salvation. All that is necessary for the sinner is to rest now by faith upon what Christ did. "The gift of God is eternal life through Jesus Christ our Lord" (Rom 6:23). To the believer, the knowledge that the atoning work of Christ is finished brings a sweet relief over against all the defects and imperfections of his services. There is nothing "finished" that we do: all our duties are imperfect. There is much of sin and vanity in the very best of our efforts, but the grand relief is that we are "complete" in Christ (Col 2:10)! Christ and His finished work are the ground of all our hopes. "It is finished."

5. Here we see the end of our sins. The sins of the believer, all of them, were transferred to the Jesus. As the Scripture says, "The Lord hath laid on him the iniquities of us all" (Isa 53:6). If then God laid my iniquities on Christ, they are no longer on me. Sin there is in me, for the old Adamic nature remains in the believer till death or till Christ's return, should He come before I die; but there is no sin on me. This distinction between sin in and sin on, is a vital one, and there should be little difficulty in apprehending it. If I were to say the judge passed sentence on a criminal, and that he is now under sentence of death, everyone would understand what I meant. In like manner, everyone out of Christ has the sentence of God's condemnation resting upon him. But when a sinner believes in the Lord Jesus, and receives Him as his Lord and Master, obey the salvation message according to (Acts 2:38-39) he is no longer "under condemnation"— sin is no longer on him, that is, the guilt, the condemnation, the penalty of sin, is no longer upon

him. And why? Because Christ bore our sins in His own body on the tree (1Pe 2:24)—the guilt, condemnation, and penalty of our sins, was transferred to our substitute. Hence, because my sins were transferred to Christ, they are no more upon me.

This precious truth was strikingly illustrated in Old Testament times regarding Israel's annual Day of Atonement. On that day, Aaron, the high priest (a type of Christ), made satisfaction to God for the sins which Israel had committed during the previous year. The way this was done is described in Leviticus 16. Two goats were taken and presented before the Lord at the door of the tabernacle: this was before anything was done with them: it represented Christ being sent and presenting Himself, offering to come into this world and be the Savior of sinners. One of the goats was then taken and killed, and its blood was carried into the tabernacle, within the veil, into the Holy of Holies, and there it was sprinkled before and upon the mercy seat—foreshadowing Christ offering Himself as a sacrifice, to meet the demands of His justice and satisfy the requirements of His holiness.

Then we read that Aaron came out of the tabernacle and laid both his hands upon the head of the second (living) goat— signifying an act of identification by which Aaron is the representative of the whole nation, identified the people with it, acknowledging that its doom was what their sins merited, and which, today, corresponds with the hands of faith laying hold of Christ and identifying ourselves with Him in His Death. Having laid his hands on the head of the live goat, Aaron now confessed over him "all the iniquities of the children of Israel, and all their transgressions in all their sins, putting them upon the head of the goat" (Lev 16:21). Thus, were Israel's sins transferred to their substitute. Finally, we are told, "And the goat shall bear upon him all their iniquities unto a land not inhabited: and he shall let go the goat in the wilderness" (Lev 16:22). The goat bearing Israel's sins, was taken unto an uninhabited wilderness, and the people of God saw him and their sins no more! In type this was Christ taking our sins into that desolate land where God was not and there making an end of them. The Cross of Christ then is the grave of our sins!

"It is finished."
6. Here we see the fulfillment of the Law's requirements. "The law is holy, and the commandment holy, and just and good" (Rom 7:12). How could it be anything less when Jehovah Himself had framed and given it! The fault lay not in the Law but in man who, being depraved and sinful, could not keep it. Yet that Law must be kept, and kept by a man, so that the Law might be honored and magnified, and its giver vindicated. Therefore, we read, "For what the law could not do, in that it was weak through the flesh, God sending his own Son, in the likeness of sinful flesh, and for sin, condemned sin in the flesh: that the righteousness of the law might be fulfilled in [not by] us, who walk not after flesh, but after the Spirit" (Rom 8:3-4). The "weakness" here is that of fallen man. The sending forth of God's Son in the likeness of sin's flesh (Greek) refers to the Incarnation: as we read in another Scripture, "God sent forth his Son, born of a woman, born under the law, that he might redeem them that were under the law" (Gal 4:4-5 RV). Yes, the Jesus was born "under the law," born under it that He might keep it perfectly in thought, word, and deed. "Think not that I am come to destroy the law, or the prophets: I am not come to destroy, but to fulfill" (Mat 5:17); such was His claim.

But not only did Jesus keep the precepts of the Law, He also suffered its penalty and endured its curse. We had broken it, and taking our place, He must receive its just sentence. Having received its penalty and endured its curse, the demands of the Law are fully met, and justice is satisfied. Therefore, is it written of believers, "Christ hath redeemed us from the curse of the law, being made a curse for us" (Gal 3:13). And again, "For Christ is the end of the law for righteousness to everyone that believeth" (Rom 10:4). And yet again, "For ye are not under the law, but under grace" (Rom 6:14). "It is finished." "Free from the Law, Jesus hath bled, and there is remission, cursed by the law and bruised by the fall, Grace hath redeemed us once for all."

7. Here we see the destruction of Satan's power. See it by faith. The Cross sounded the death of the devil's power. To human appearances it looked like the moment of his greatest triumph, yet, it was the hour of his ultimate defeat. In view of the Cross Jesus declared, "Now is the judgment of this world: now shall the prince of this world be cast out" (Joh 12:31). It is true that Satan has not yet been chained and cast into the bottomless pit, nevertheless, sentence has been passed (though not yet executed); his doom is certain; and his power is already broken so far as believers are concerned.

For the Christian, the devil is a vanquished foe. He was defeated by Christ at the Cross— "that through death he might destroy him that had the power of death, that is, the devil" (Hebrew 2:14). Believers have already been "delivered from the power of darkness" and translated into the kingdom of God's dear Son (Col 1:13). Satan, then, should be treated as a defeated enemy. No longer has he any legitimate claim upon us. Once we were his lawful "captives"; but now God worketh in us both to will and to do of His good pleasure. All that we now must do is to "resist the devil," and the promise is, "he will flee from you" (James 4:7).

"It is finished." Here was the triumphant answer to the rage of man and the enmity of Satan. It tells of the perfect work which meets sin in the place of judgment. All was completed just as God would have it, just as the prophets had foretold, just as the Old Testament ceremonial had foreshadowed, just as divine holiness demanded, and just as sinners needed. How strikingly appropriate is this sixth Cross-utterance of Jesus found in John's Gospel—the Gospel which displays the glory of Christ's deity! He seals it with His own words, attesting it is complete, and giving it the all-sufficient sanction of His own approval. Jesus says, "It is finished"—who then dare doubt or question it.

"It is finished." Reader, do you believe it? or, are you trying to add something of your own to the finished work of Christ to secure the favor of God? All you must do is to accept the pardon which He purchased. God is satisfied with His work on the cross, why are not you? Sinner, the moment you believe Jesus' testimony that it is finished, that moment every sin you have committed is blotted out, and you stand accepted in Christ! O would you not like to possess the assurance that there is nothing between your soul and God? Would you not like to know that every sin had been atoned for and put away? Then believe what God's Word says about Christ's death. Rest not on your feelings and experiences but on the written Word. There is only one way of finding peace, deliverance, wholeness, salvation, victory over the "it" and that is through faith in the shed blood of Jesus the of Lamb God. It is time to "Get Rid of "it", Before "it" Gets Rid of You".

"It is finished." Do you really believe it? Or, are you endeavoring to add something of your own to it and thus merit the favor of God? By continuing to hold on and struggle, seeking other sources to deal with the "it" in your life, you are nullifying the finished work of Christ by your own miserable additions to it!". The Gospel of God's grace, and the finished work of Christ is sufficient for our souls to rest upon. In the pages of this book, God uses forceful object lessons and His Word to show you, "How to Get Rid of "it", before "it" Gets Rid of You". It is a grave mistake not to embrace the Word of God, and cast yourself by faith upon what Christ had done for you.

Victory was given to us by way of the cross. Whatever your "it" or "its" might be, "it" has come to kill, steal and destroy you. Make a conscious effort to explore this information given in this book and expose the enemy of your soul. Let's "Get Rid of "it". After all, "It is Finished"

CHAPTER ONE

What is "it"?

We are all created with a basic need to be loved. God created us to both give and receive love, but though damaged emotions, our capacity to receive love can be dramatically hindered. Ignorance of God's love will also hinder us from receiving the great and glorious love that He has for us. **The root of most "its" is a lack of love being received by that person.** Many of us have been damaged emotionally by rejection, abandonment, abuse, etc., and thereby our capacity to receive love has been reduced. **Only an emotionally healthy person is capable of both giving and receiving love as God intended.**

Self-worth issues can hinder love

Self-worth issues are rooted in believing that we are not worthy or deserve to be loved. When we believe that we are unlovable, we will unconsciously reject any love that comes our way. We won't believe the love, because we believe in our hearts that we are not worthy. **Self-worth issues are all rooted in our failing to see who we really are in Christ.**

If you walked into a gallery of world-class art, and pointed to a painting, saying, "That is the ugliest thing I've ever seen! Who painted that??" Now let's say the artist was standing right next to you. How do you think that would make him feel? Do you realize we are the artwork of God, a special painting crafted together by the master painter? Do you think it brings Him honor when we look down on ourselves? **We need to stop putting down what God has made.**

Many times, we have self-unforgiveness issues because we blame ourselves for something, or we've done something we deeply regret, and we simply cannot let it go. We need to realize that Jesus has forgiven us of all our failures, and we need to start seeing ourselves as forgiven. Otherwise, we're denying the work of Christ in our life! **If God forgave you, and you're still beating yourself up, then you don't really believe what Jesus did for you.** It's that simple!

Just as we must forgive others (see Matthew 18:21-35), we need to forgive ourselves just the same. Self-hate has been known to be the root behind diseases such as lupus and Crohn's disease, as well as other auto-immune diseases. We need to stop holding ourselves accountable for that which Jesus has set us free from.

If we want to be in faith, we need to BELIEVE what Jesus did for us, and part of that believing is seeing ourselves as forgiven and clothed with the righteousness of God, which is upon all who believe in the finished work of Christ. Without faith, it is impossible to please God (see Hebrews 11:6), so if you want to please God, start taking the finished work of the cross seriously, and begin to see yourself as forgiven, washed clean, and clothed in the righteousness of God. For the righteousness (right standing with God) is upon all who believe:

> *"Even the righteousness of God which is by faith of Jesus Christ unto all and upon all them that believe..." (Romans 3:22 KJV)*

Unforgiveness is rooted in a lack of realization of how much God has forgiven us, and therefore we're not thankful for the steep and terrible price that Jesus paid for our own failures. Therefore, it is so important to mediate on what Jesus did for us, until it transforms our heart. The message of Jesus' work for us is what causes faith to arise in our hearts and transforms us from the inside out (read Romans 10:8-17).

Learning to see yourself as God sees you, and forgive yourself because you want to please God and be in faith and be thankful for what Jesus did for you, is the biggest step in overcoming self-worth issues. Of course, there are spirits that may need to be driven out as well, such as self-hate, guilt, condemnation, etc.

Receiving the love God has for us

When it comes to God's love for us, that's obvious, considering how He loves even the sinner so much that Jesus came to die for them. Anybody who knows the message of the cross, has some knowledge of God's love for us. However, many times, we blame God for our problems, and so we don't believe the love that He has for us. Not only do we blame Him for our problems, many times we think that God gave us the sickness or problem in our life to teach us something. Nothing could be further from the truth! Jesus tells us clearly who came to kill, steal, and destroy, and who came so that we could have life and have it in abundance.

> *"The thief cometh not, but for to steal, and to kill, and to destroy: I am come that they might have life, and that they might have it more abundantly." (John 10:10 KJV)*

If we are going to receive the love that God has for us, we need to get our thinking straightened out. He's not the one behind our problems, but rather Jesus paid the full price so that we can be forgiven all our sins, both physically and emotionally healed, and blessed.

> *"When the even was come, they brought unto him many that were possessed with devils: and he cast out the spirits with his word, and healed all that were*

Look at how good God's heart is toward mankind! Not only did Jesus heal them, but He proved the blessings of the covenant we have with Him today concerning our healing and deliverance. Isn't He good toward us? **The reason why things happen to us, is because we live in a fallen world that is under the control of the evil one.** It's not God's fault. He loves you. Jesus died for you.

Settling the fact that God loves you and is good toward you is crucial to restoring your God-given capacity to receive His love. If you can't receive His love, then you need to stop and ask yourself four questions:

1. Am I blaming God for anything bad that happened to me?

2. Have I been emotionally wounded in such a way that it is hindering my ability to freely receive love as God intended me to?

3. Do I have knowledge and revelation of how much God loves me? Do I have a solid Biblical understanding of how I am loved with the same kind of love that the Father has for Jesus?

4. Is there a self-worth issue that makes me feel unworthy to be loved?

Settling these issues lays a foundation for breaking free from the power of the "IT". You must repair the damage and faulty thinking which hinders your ability to receive the love that God has for you.

How do you know if you are receiving God's love or if it's hindered? **If you are not passionate about Jesus, then somewhere your ability to receive His love is hindered.**

If you are living a life without receiving God's love in your heart daily, you are missing out on the most fulfilling life you can have here on this earth. To know God's love, which surpasses all understanding (see Philippians 4:7), dispels all our fears and gives us a sense of peace and joy that we could never otherwise know.

"And we have known and believed the love that God hath to us. God is love; and he that dwelleth in love dwelleth in God, and God in him. Herein is our love made perfect, that we may have boldness in the day of judgment: because as he is, so are we in this world. There is no fear in love; but perfect love casteth out fear: because fear hath torment. He that feareth is not made perfect in love." (1 John 4:16-18 KJV)

What exactly is "it'?

An "it" is formed when we try to use something other than God, to meet our need to be loved. When our ability to receive God's love into our hearts is hindered, we will feel like something is missing, and seek to fill that void with something else. When that thing, whatever it might be, fills that void, we grow to love "it" because it's meeting a need. Over time, we establish a relationship with that thing, and when it comes time to depart, it's like breaking up a relationship. That's why the "it" is so destructive; we've relied on that thing to meet a need and we've established a relationship with it. Now when it's time to break up the love, it isn't so easy to say goodbye.

One widespread problem that we see when we try to deal with "it", is where we give up one "it" successfully, only to find yourself with another "it". We might quit drinking only to start overeating, for example. We might think we're finding victory, but all we're really doing is trading one "it" for another "it". This is because something must fill the love-void in our hearts, and if it's not one thing, it will be another.

What about cutting or self-harm?

Cutting or self-mutation is a special type of "it", where there's a need to either release pain in a person's heart or the person believes that they deserve to be punished for their failures. In these cases, the person certainly has an issue receiving the love that God has for them but there's another type of root that needs to be addressed as well. There's emotional pain or guilt that the person is dealing with that needs to be resolved. Finding out what happened and receiving Christ's truth concerning those areas is important for their healing. Any bondage involving guilt will need to be resolved through realizing and accepting the work of Christ on the cross for that person and they will likely need spirits of guilt, condemnation, self-hate, etc. driven out in Jesus' name. Again, getting the person to see them self for who they really are in Christ, forgiven, loved, and blessed, is crucial to lasting freedom from self-hate issues.

See yourself as lovable!

The key in uprooting most "its" is to deal with the underlying issues which are limiting their capacity to freely receive love from God and others, along with dealing with any self-worth issues by establishing an understanding of your true identity in Christ. **Coming to a place where you believe you are lovable is key to receiving love in general**, so dealing with self-worth issues is an important key to breaking down the walls which keep us from feeling loved. The only way to obtain a true sense of worth and value is to get a revelation of how much you are loved by God, who sent His son Jesus to die for you.

Discovering the root

To discover the root of your "it", you need to get real honest with yourself. Many times, we are in denial about the pain we are feeling. Figuring out what is the root of a bondage is all about asking the right questions, and that is especially important when it comes to uprooting an "it". Why don't we feel loved? Do we feel unlovable? (Let's stop right there; if we feel unlovable, then you've just discovered a self-worth issue that will need to be addressed.) Are you passionate about Jesus? If not, then something in hindering you from realizing how much you are loved by Him who died for you. Do you see yourself as forgiven and loved by the God because of what He did for you?

As you discover emotional wounds, you'll need to forgive (others, yourself, and God) and invite Jesus to come and heal the damage in your heart. If you don't realize how much God loves you, then you'll need to spend some time learning about what Jesus did for you on the cross, and what a terrible price He paid because He loved you so very much. Often breaking out of an "it" is a combination of emotional healing, learning about who you are in Christ, forgiving (yourself, others, and God), overcoming self-worth issues by changing how you see yourself (in light of how God sees and loves you), and casting out any spirits that came in and are enforcing the destructive behavior. Spirits behind guilt, condemnation, etc. also need to be driven out, as they seek to keep us from fully seeing what Jesus did for us on the cross.

Dealing with the issues underlying an "it" is key to uprooting it permanently. If you want lasting freedom and wholeness in this area of your life, you will have to deal with the issues that have limited your capacity to receive love, especially the love that God has for you.

CHAPTER TWO

The "it" of Anxiety and Worry

DEFINITION: Anxiety is the state of being troubled with fearful, distressing thoughts and worrying about real or imagined problems.

FACTS ABOUT ANXIETY AND WORRY:

Anxiety and worry express unbelief. Anxiety and worry are manifestations of a carnal nature expressing doubts in the ability of God to handle situations.

Anxiety and worry do not change anything. Through fretful thoughts you cannot add one hour to your life, so why worry? (Luke 12:25-26).

Anxiety and worry affect your health. Anxious, worried people may suffer nervousness, sleeplessness, headaches, and panic attacks--the long-term effects of which can affect vital organs.

Anxiety causes you to lose spiritual focus. Anxiety changes your focus from the eternal to the temporal. Your focus is to be on the Kingdom of God, not the things of the world (Matthew 6:28-34). The Bible warns, *"Be careful, or your hearts will be weighed down with dissipation, drunkenness and the anxieties of life, and that day will close on you unexpectedly like a trap" (Luke 21:34).* "That day" is speaking of end-time events and return of the Lord.

DEALING WITH ANXIETY AND WORRY:

Ask God for forgiveness. Anxiety and worry reflect unbelief that God is able to handle the situations in your life. Ask forgiveness for unbelief.

Address why you are anxious and worried. Like David, question yourself: *"Why are you downcast, O my soul? Why so disturbed within me?"* Then, whatever the reason for your concern, tell yourself by faith: *"Put your hope in God, for I will yet praise him, my Savior and my God. My soul is downcast within me; therefore, I will remember you ..." (Psalm 42:5-6)*

Boldly declare that the Lord will help in any situation causing worry. He is your source of strength (Philippians 4:13). *"So, we take comfort and are encouraged and confidently and boldly say, The Lord is my helper, I will not be seized with alarm-I will not fear or dread or be terrified. What can man do to me?" (Heb. 13:6, TAB).*

Cast your cares on God. The Bible says to cast your cares on the Lord (Psalm 55:22). The word "cast" implies a continuous action. You may cast your cares on God, yet anxious thoughts return. When they do, cast again!

Pray and praise God instead of thinking anxious thoughts. The Word says: *"Do not be anxious about anything, but in everything, by prayer and petition, with thanksgiving, present your requests to God. And the peace of God, which transcends all understanding, will guard your hearts and your minds in Christ Jesus" (Philippians 4:6-7).* Turn every anxious thought into a prayer, then praise God for the answer.

Do not worry. This is a command, not an option (Luke 12:22-23). Worry is focused on the future, and Jesus said not to think about tomorrow (Matthew 6:34). God designed the world to run on a 24-hour schedule. Don't violate this principle by worrying about the future.

Replace worry with the Word. The Word of God is effective in dealing with worry and anxiety. Following are some excerpts to get you started. In addition, go through your Bible and mark all of the promises of God and His faithfulness. Review these when you are tempted to worry.

WHAT GOD'S WORD SAYS ABOUT ANXIETY AND WORRY:

Do not fret--it leads only to evil. (Psalm 37:8)

Why are you downcast, O my soul? Why so disturbed within me? Put your hope in God, for I will yet praise him, my Savior and my God. My soul is downcast within me; therefore, I will remember you ... (Psalm 42:5-6)

Cast your cares on the Lord and he will sustain you; he will never let the righteous fall. (Psalm 55:22)

When anxiety was great within me, your consolation brought joy to my soul. (Psalm 94:19)

An anxious heart weighs a man down, but a kind word cheers him up. (Proverbs 12:25)

The wicked man flees though no one pursues, but the righteous are as bold as a lion. (Proverbs 28:1)

And why do you worry about clothes? See how the lilies of the field grow. They do not labor or spin. Yet I tell you that not even Solomon in all his splendor was dressed like one of these. If that is how God clothes the grass of the field, which is here today and tomorrow is thrown into the fire, will he not much more clothe you, O you of little faith? So do not worry, saying, 'What shall we eat?' or 'What shall we drink?' or 'What shall we wear?' For the pagans run after all these things, and your heavenly Father knows that you need them. But seek first his kingdom and his righteousness, and all these things will be given to you as well. Therefore, do not worry about tomorrow, for tomorrow will worry about itself. Each day has enough trouble of its own. (Matthew 6:28-34)

Therefore, I tell you, do not worry about your life, what you will eat; or about your body, what you will wear. Life is more than food and the body more than clothes. (Luke 12:22-23)

Who of you by worrying can add a single hour to his life? Since you cannot do this very little thing, why do you worry about the rest? (Luke 12:25-26)

Be careful, or your hearts will be weighed down with dissipation, drunkenness and the anxieties of life, and that day will close on you unexpectedly like a trap. (Luke 21:34)

Do not be anxious about anything, but in everything, by prayer and petition, with thanksgiving, present your requests to God. And the peace of God, which transcends all understanding, will guard your hearts and your minds in Christ Jesus. (Philippians 4:6-7)

Cast all your anxiety on him because he cares for you. (1 Peter 5:7)

CHAPTER THREE

The "it" of Inferiority

DEFINITION: Inferiority is a belief that you are not as good as or of less value than other people. You feel that you continuously fail to meet standards of quality, ability, or achievement. Inferiority is a lack of self-worth and self-respect.

FACTS ABOUT INFERIORITY:

Everyone feels inferior at times. Moses felt inferior for the task to which he was called (Exodus 3:11-12). Jeremiah felt too immature to fulfill God's plan (Jeremiah 1:6-7). Gideon thought he was the least of all in the tribe of Israel (Judges 6:15). The great Apostle Paul confessed to weakness, fear, and trembling (1 Corinthians 2:3). The nation of Israel saw themselves as grasshoppers in the eyes of their powerful enemies (Numbers 13:33). Often, when you are out of the "comfort zone" of your environment, friends, and family, you may feel inferior or inept.

The causes of inferiority may include your physical appearance, your abilities, social adaptability, and the environment from which you come. Your parents may have instilled inferiority feelings through constant criticism. Continual failure can also breed feelings of inferiority--you just never seem to succeed like other people. Satan also causes feelings of inferiority, as he constantly brings accusations against God's people (Revelation 12:10).

Fear is related to inferiority. The fear of others and the fear of failure contribute to inferiority. (See "Fear" in this database for guidelines on overcoming fear.)

Inferiority can lead to destructive behaviors. If you think you aren't worth much, then it can lead to destructive behaviors such as sexual promiscuity, addictions, self-mutilation, etc.

Inferiority is a feeling. Faith is a fact. As a believer, you live by faith and not by feelings. You must, by faith, believe you are who God says you are rather than believe what your feelings dictate.

God does not accept inferiority as an excuse. When the prophet Jeremiah said he felt too immature to accomplish God's purposes, the Lord rebuked him (Jeremiah 1:6-8).

DEALING WITH INFERIORITY:

Realize that you are created in the image of God. He created mankind in His image and declared His creation to be good. (Genesis 1;26-31).

See yourself as God sees you. If you are a believer, God sees you as a son or daughter, and a joint heir with Jesus Christ (Galatians 4:6-7). It is not self-esteem that should be your focus, rather it is Godlike esteem--who you are because of who He is within and through you.

Do not compare yourself to others. Many feelings of inferiority arise when you compare yourself to others. The Bible indicates this is not wise (2 Corinthians 10:12).

Live by faith and not by feeling. Romans 1:17 declares *"For in the gospel a righteousness from God is revealed, a righteousness that is by faith from first to last, just as it is written: "The righteous will live by faith."*

Don't dwell on your past. Do not focus on past failures to live up to your own expectations or those of others. God says: *"Forget the former things; do not dwell on the past. See, I am doing a new thing! Now it springs up; do you not perceive it?" (Isaiah 43:18-19).*

Avoid friends who pull you down. Seek friends who encourage your efforts and accept you as you are--a work in progress.

Control your thoughts. Do not allow thoughts of inferiority to remain in your mind. When they try to enter, reject them immediately. (See "Mind and Thoughts" in this database for guidelines for controlling your thoughts.)

Confess sufficiency in God. Confess Philippians 4:13: *"I can do everything through him who gives me strength."* It is not who you are, but who you are in God that is important.

Learn from the lives of biblical characters who felt inferior. Moses, Gideon, Jeremiah, the Apostle Paul, and the nation of Israel are examples of people who had inferior feelings, yet rose above them to become mighty people of God. You can do the same!

WHAT GOD'S WORD SAYS ABOUT INFERIORITY:

Forget the former things; do not dwell on the past. See, I am doing a new thing! Now it springs up; do you not perceive it? (Isaiah 43:18-19).

"Ah, Sovereign Lord," I said, "I do not know how to speak; I am only a child." But the Lord said to me, "Do not say, 'I am only a child.' You must go to everyone I send you to and say whatever I command you. Do not be afraid of them, for I am with you and will rescue you," declares the Lord." (Jeremiah 1:6-8)

For in the gospel a righteousness from God is revealed, a righteousness that is by faith from first to last, just as it is written: "The righteous will live by faith *(not feeling)*. (Romans 1:17)

We do not dare to classify or compare ourselves with some who commend themselves. When they measure themselves by themselves and compare themselves with themselves, they are not wise. (2 Corinthians 10:12)

Because you are sons, God sent the Spirit of his Son into our hearts, the Spirit who calls out, "Abba, Father." So you are no longer a slave, but a son; and since you are a son, God has made you also an heir. (Galatians 4:6-7)

I can do everything through him who gives me strength. (Philippians 4:13)

Don't let anyone look down on you because you are young, but set an example for the believers in speech, in life, in love, in faith and in purity. (1 Timothy 4:12)

But you are a chosen people, a royal priesthood, a holy nation, a people belonging to God, that you may declare the praises of him who called you out of darkness into his wonderful light. (1 Peter 2:9)

CHAPTER FOUR

The "it" of Confusion

DEFINITION: Confusion is a lack of clarity or a misunderstanding of the truth or facts in a given situation. It is disruption in regards to time, place, people, or tasks to be accomplished.

FACTS ABOUT CONFUSION:

God is not the author of confusion. God does not cause confusion. If He does not cause it, then it is obvious that it is caused by Satan (1 Corinthians 14:33).

The causes of confusion. Evil spiritual powers may try to cause confusion. Confusion may also be caused by sin in your life, by looking to man instead of God, by lack of knowledge of the truth of God' Word, and an inability to hear God's voice and know His will. Your inability to hear God's voice often arises from neglecting prayer and study of the Word. You do not stay in His presence long enough to receive His direction. Confusion also results simply because you do not ask for wisdom from God.

You never need be confused. You can ask for wisdom from God for every situation in life and you will receive it (James 3:14-17).

The Holy Spirit is your guide. If you are a born-again, Spirit-filled believer, then the Holy Spirit is resident within you.   One of His purposes is to guide you into all truth so that you need never be confused.

DEALING WITH CONFUSION:

Discover the root cause of confusion. Is it simply because of miscommunication or is it due to demonic powers? Is it because you have not sought God's will concerning the situation with which you are dealing? Deal with the root causes of the confusion.

Reject the spirit of confusion. Confusion is a spirit. Do not allow it to operate in your life. Anytime confusion starts to arise in your circumstances, stop and rebuke it immediately!

Resist the devil. Satan causes confusion, so submit yourself to God, resist Satan, and he will flee from you (James 4:7)

Ask God for wisdom. The Bible says: *"If any of you lacks wisdom, he should ask God, who gives generously to all without finding fault, and it will be given to him" (James 1:5).*

Embrace and act upon the truth. Jesus said: *"If you hold to my teaching, you are really my disciples. Then you will know the truth, and the truth will set you free" (John 8:31-32).* Reject the lies of Satan that bring confusion and embrace God's truth.

WHAT GOD'S WORD SAYS ABOUT CONFUSION:

In thee, oh Lord, do I put my trust: let me never be put to confusion. (Psalm 71:1, KJV)

A man's steps are directed by the Lord. How then can anyone understand his own way? (Proverbs 20:24)

The statutes of the Lord are trustworthy, making wise the simple. (Psalm 19:7)

The unfolding of your words gives light; it gives understanding to the simple. (Psalm 119:130)

For we know in part and we prophesy in part, but when perfection comes, the imperfect disappears. (1 Corinthians 13:9-10)

There is nothing concealed that will not be disclosed, or hidden that will not be made known. (Luke 12:2)

Now we see but a poor reflection as in a mirror; then we shall see face to face. Now I know in part; then I shall know fully, even as I am fully known. (1 Corinthians 13:12)

If you hold to my teaching, you are really my disciples. Then you will know the truth, and the truth will set you free. (John 8:31-32)

But the Counselor, the Holy Spirit, whom the Father will send in my name, will teach you all things and will remind you of everything I have said to you. (John 14:26)

If any of you lacks wisdom, he should ask God, who gives generously to all without finding fault, and it will be given to him. (James 1:5)

We know also that the Son of God has come and has given us understanding, so that we may know him who is true. (1 John 5:20)

CHAPTER FIVE

The "it" of Depression
(Disappointment and Discouragement)

DEFINITIONS: Depression is an emotional condition characterized by feelings of continued hopelessness, inadequacy, gloom, dejection, sadness, and difficulty in thinking, concentration, and action. Depression also causes loss of interest, hopelessness, and, in some cases, thoughts of suicide. Discouragement and disappointment often result in depression.

FACTS ABOUT DEPRESSION:

Both positive and negative circumstances contribute to depression. A great loss, death of a loved one, losing a job, traumatic experiences, divorce, imprisonment, financial problems and other negative circumstances can cause depression. Guilt is another trigger for depression, and struggles with addictions can cause it. Discouragement and disappointment are related emotions also. But positive circumstances may also cause depression: A new job, geographic relocation, retirement, a new baby. These are positive things, but they produce levels of stress that can result in depression.

Depression is caused by negative emotional responses to circumstances, physical or mental conditions, or attacks by Satan on your mind.

Disappointment in others contributes to depression. People disappoint you and don't measure up to what you want from them. Jesus told Peter not to be concerned about the performance or destiny of others (John 21:23). The Apostle Paul declared: *"We do not dare to classify or compare ourselves with some who commend themselves. When they measure themselves by themselves and compare themselves with themselves, they are not wise" (2 Corinthians 10:12).*

Discouragement may be caused by difficult circumstances. Poor health, financial problems, relationship issues, etc., can cause discouragement that leads to a diminished joy in life.

Unconfessed sin also contributes to depression (Psalm 38:38).

Errant spiritual decisions cause depression. The rich young man who refused to put all he had into the hands of Jesus went away "sorrowing" (Mark 10:22). Sometimes the root of depression is a spiritual cause--a refusal to place some aspect of our lives, abilities, possessions, family and friends, or sorrows into the hands of the Lord.

Depression can affect anyone. Male and female, young and old--even children and teenagers can be depressed.

Depression affects every aspect of your being--spiritually, mentally, emotionally, and physically. It can cause a change in your sleeping patterns, weight changes, loss of appetite or overeating, loss of interest in sex, lack of energy, problems with concentration, poor memory, and difficulty in making decisions. Emotionally it causes low-self-image, self-criticism, hopelessness, anger, resentment, guilt, irritability, crying, fear, gloomy outlook. You may

29

withdraw from social relationships and your work ethic may be affected. You may also be tempted to turn to drugs and alcohol--which only tend to further the depression.

Depression can lead to suicide. If depression is not dealt with, it can lead to such hopelessness that a person contemplates or tries suicide to escape the pain. (See "Suicide" in this database.)

Depression is not sin. It is a signal that change, a healing, or deliverance is needed in your life.

DEALING WITH DEPRESSION:

Identify the root cause. How did the depression begin? When did it begin? What is the main issue causing it? Is your depression because of finances? Loneliness? Unconfessed sin? Are negative emotions causing it--things like anger and unforgiveness? Physical problems? An attack of Satan on your mind?

If unconfessed sin is the problem, ask God for forgiveness. David said that day and night, God's hand was heavy on him until he asked for forgiveness. Ask God to forgive your negative thinking and wrong emotions. If you are harboring unforgiveness, forgive!

Have a medical examination if you think your health is affecting your mood. If it is a medical condition, you can then pray for physical healing rather than misdirecting your efforts by thinking you are fighting a battle of the mind over depression.

Take these steps if your depression is due to negative circumstances and/or attacks of Satan:

> -Pray and bind the spirit of depression that is operating in your life. Jesus gave you power over all the power of the enemy, and that includes depression (Luke 10:19).

> -Eliminate drugs and alcohol--they only contribute to depression.

> -Reprogram your thinking by immersing yourself in God's Word. The Word of God can change every area of your life--physically, mentally, emotionally, and spiritually. Program your mind to think on good things rather than the negative (Philippians 4:8).

> -Do not look at your circumstances. Keep your focus on God.

> -Recognize that God's ultimate purpose is to do you good and that He is in control of your circumstances (Jeremiah 29:11).

-When depressing thoughts try to return, resist the devil in the name of Jesus and he will flee (James 4:7). How you react to these thoughts is the key to your deliverance, as the battle of depression is in the mind. As long as you allow yourself to think you are defeated and depressed, you will remain that way because... *"As he thinks in his heart, so is he..." (Proverbs 23:7, NKJV)*. Remember that with every temptation you face, there is a way of escape (1 Corinthians 10:13).

-Encourage yourself in the Lord. Read 1 Samuel chapter 30 to see how David encouraged himself during a tragic event in his life. Read the book of Psalms and you will note that David is often discouraged, but finds encouragement in God.

-Praise and worship the Lord. Satan hates praise and worship and will flee in the presence of your sacrifice of praise.

Get proper rest, sleep, exercise, and nutrition. These all help with the physical aspects of depression.

Make positive changes in your life. What changes can you make that will eliminate stress? What changes will bring joy back into your life?

Return to the basics of Christian life. Be faithful in prayer, church attendance, and the Word of God. These will encourage you and give you a more positive attitude. The Word of God is effective to facilitate change in any problem or circumstance of your life. Depression is a state of mind, and your mind can be renewed through the Word (Ephesians 4:23; Colossians 3:10).

Cultivate friendships with positive people. Avoid being a loner. Satan wants to isolate you through depression. Deliberately spend time with believers who are positive and uplifting. Do not hang out with negative, critical, judgmental people, as this can contribute to your depressed state. Christian friendships with positive people will help you when you are feeling down (Ecclesiastes 4:9-10).

Do something for others. This will take the focus off of yourself and the joy you receive from doing acts of kindness can help your own depression.

Start a gratitude journal. Write down at least one thing each day for which you are thankful. This will help you focus on the positive instead of the negative.

WHAT GOD'S WORD SAYS ABOUT DEPRESSION:

The Lord himself goes before you and will be with you; he will never leave you nor forsake you. Do not be afraid; do not be discouraged. (Deuteronomy 31:8)

But you are a shield around me, O Lord; you bestow glory on me and lift up my head. (Psalm 3:3)

The Lord is a refuge for the oppressed, a stronghold in times of trouble. Those who know your name will trust in you, for you, Lord, have never forsaken those who seek you. (Psalm 9:9-10)

I am still confident of this: I will see the goodness of the Lord in the land of the living. Wait for the Lord; be strong and take heart and wait for the Lord. (Psalm 27:13-14)

The Lord is my strength and my shield; my heart trusts in him, and I am helped. My heart leaps for joy and I will give thanks to him in song. (Psalm 28:7)

The Lord is close to the brokenhearted and saves those who are crushed in spirit. (Psalm 34:18)

Read Psalm 38 as an example of depression caused by personal sin. Read Psalm 51, a prayer of repentance which restored the joy of salvation to David.

I waited patiently for the Lord; he turned to me and heard my cry. He lifted me out of the slimy pit, out of the mud and mire; he set my feet on a rock and gave me a firm place to stand. He put a new song in my mouth, a hymn of praise to our God. Many will see and fear and put their trust in the Lord. (Psalm 40:1-3)

Why are you downcast, O my soul? Why so disturbed within me? Put your hope in God, for I will yet praise him, my Savior and my God. (Psalm 42:5, 11; 43:5)

God is our refuge and strength, an ever-present help in trouble. Therefore, we will not fear, though the earth gives way and the mountains fall into the heart of the sea, though its waters roar and foam and the mountains quake with their surging. (Psalm 46:1-3)

Cast your cares on the Lord and he will sustain you; he will never let the righteous fall. (Psalm 55:22)

Find rest, O my soul, in God alone; my hope comes from him. (Psalm 62:5)

When I said, "My foot is slipping," your love, O Lord, supported me. When anxiety was great within me, your consolation brought joy to my soul. (Psalm 94:18-19)

Even in darkness light dawns for the upright, for the gracious and compassionate and righteous man.   (Psalm 112:4)

Though I walk in the midst of trouble, you will revive me; You will stretch out Your hand Against the wrath of my enemies, And Your right hand will save me. (Psalm 138:7, NKJV)

The Lord upholds all those who fall and lifts up all who are bowed down. (Psalm 145:14

He heals the brokenhearted and binds up their wounds. (Psalm 147:3)

Trust in the Lord with all your heart and lean not on your own understanding; in all your ways acknowledge him, and he will make your paths straight.   (Proverbs 3:5-6)

An anxious heart weighs a man down, but a kind word cheers him up. (Proverbs 12:25)

The spirit of a man will sustain him in sickness, but who can bear a broken spirit?

(Proverbs 18:14)

Two are better than one, because they have a good return for their work: If one falls down, his friend can help him up. But pity the man who falls and has no one to help him up! (Ecclesiastes 4:9-10).

Anyone who is among the living has hope. (Ecclesiastes 9:4)

You will keep in perfect peace him whose mind is steadfast, because he trusts in you. (Isaiah 26:3)

But those who hope in the Lord will renew their strength. They will soar on wings like eagles; they will run and not grow weary, they will walk and not be faint. (Isaiah 40:31)

Fear not, for I am with you; Be not dismayed, for I am your God. I will strengthen you, Yes, I will help you, I will uphold you with My righteous right hand. (Isaiah 41:10)

...Fear not, for I have redeemed you; I have summoned you by name; you are mine. When you pass through the waters, I will be with you; and when you pass through the rivers, they will not sweep over you. When you walk through the fire, you will not be burned; the flames will not set you ablaze. (Isaiah 43:1-2)

Surely, he took up our infirmities and carried our sorrows, yet we considered him stricken by God, smitten by him, and afflicted. But he was pierced for our transgressions, he was crushed for our iniquities; the punishment that brought us peace was upon him, and by his wounds we are healed. (Isaiah 53:4-5)

Arise, shine, for your light has come, and the glory of the Lord rises upon you. See, darkness covers the earth and thick darkness is over the peoples, but the Lord rises upon you and his glory appears over you. (Isaiah 60:1)

"For I know the thoughts that I think toward you," says the Lord, "thoughts of peace and not of evil, to give you a future and a hope." (Jeremiah 29:11, NKJV)

The Lord is good, a refuge in times of trouble. (Nahum 1:7)

Come to me, all you who are weary and burdened, and I will give you rest. Take my yoke upon you and learn from me, for I am gentle and humble in heart, and you will find rest for your souls. For my yoke is easy and my burden is light. (Matthew 11:28-30)

I have given you authority to trample on snakes and scorpions and to overcome all the power of the enemy; nothing will harm you. (Luke 10:19)

The thief comes only to steal and kill and destroy; I have come that they may have life, and have it to the full. (John 10:10)

Peace I leave with you; my peace I give you. I do not give to you as the world gives. Do not let your hearts be troubled and do not be afraid. (John14:27)

I have told you these things, so that in me you may have peace. In this world you will have trouble. But take heart! I have overcome the world.   (John 16:33)

I consider that our present sufferings are not worth comparing with the glory that will be revealed in us. (Romans 8:18-22)

And we know that in all things God works for the good of those who love him, who have been called according to his purpose. (Romans 8:28-29)

Who shall separate us from the love of Christ? Shall trouble or hardship or persecution or famine or nakedness or danger or sword? As it is written: "For your sake we face death all day long; we are considered as sheep to be slaughtered."   No, in all these things we are more than conquerors through him who loved us. For I am convinced that neither death nor life, neither angels nor demons, neither the present nor the future, nor any powers, neither height nor depth, nor anything else in all creation, will be able to separate us from the love of God that is in Christ Jesus our Lord. (Romans 8:35-39)

Therefore, I urge you, brothers, in view of God's mercy, to offer your bodies as living sacrifices, holy and pleasing to God--this is your spiritual act of worship. Do not conform any longer to the pattern of this world, but be transformed by the renewing of your mind. Then you will be able to test and approve what God's will is--his good, pleasing and perfect will. (Romans 12:2)

No temptation has seized you except what is common to man. And God is faithful; he will not let you be tempted beyond what you can bear. But when you are tempted, he will also provide a way out so that you can stand up under it. (1 Corinthians 10:13)

We are hard pressed on every side, but not crushed; perplexed, but not in despair; persecuted, but not abandoned; struck down, but not destroyed. (2 Corinthians 4:8-9)

For though we live in the world, we do not wage war as the world does. The weapons we fight with are not the weapons of the world. On the contrary, they have divine power to demolish strongholds. We demolish arguments and every pretension that sets itself up against the knowledge of God, and we take captive every thought to make it obedient to Christ. (2 Corinthians 10:3-5)

And let us not grow weary while doing good, for in due season we shall reap if we do not lose heart. (Galatians 6:9, NKJV)

Rejoice in the Lord always. I will say it again: Rejoice! Let your gentleness be evident to all. The Lord is near. Do not be anxious about anything, but in everything, by prayer and petition, with thanksgiving, present your requests to God. And the peace of God, which transcends all understanding, will guard your hearts and your minds in Christ Jesus. Finally, brothers, whatever is true, whatever is noble, whatever is right, whatever is pure, whatever is lovely, whatever is admirable--if anything is excellent or praiseworthy--think about such things. Whatever you have learned or received or heard from me, or seen in me--put it into practice. And the God of peace will be with you. (Philippians 4:4--9)

For God did not give us a spirit of timidity, but a spirit of power, of love and of self-discipline. (2 Timothy 1:7)

For we do not have a High Priest who cannot sympathize with our weaknesses, but was in all points tempted as we are, yet without sin. Let us therefore come boldly to the throne of grace, that we may obtain mercy and find grace to help in time of need. (Hebrews 4:15-16, NKJV)

Blessed is the man who perseveres under trial, because when he has stood the test, he will receive the crown of life that God has promised to those who love him. When tempted, no one should say, "God is tempting me." For God cannot be tempted by evil, nor does he tempt anyone; but each one is tempted when, by his own evil desire, he is dragged away and enticed. Then, after desire has conceived, it gives birth to sin; and sin, when it is full-grown, gives birth to death. Don't be deceived, my dear brothers. Every good and perfect gift is from above, coming down from the Father of the heavenly lights, who does not change like shifting shadows. (James 1:12-17)

Submit yourselves, then, to God. Resist the devil, and he will flee from you. (James 4:7-8)

He himself bore our sins in his body on the tree, so that we might die to sins and live for righteousness; by his wounds you have been healed. (1 Peter 2:24)

Study the story of the Prophet Elijah's depression in 1 Kings 18-19.

CHAPTER SIX

The "it" of Doubt

DEFINITION: Doubt is a lack of assurance that causes one to question their salvation as well as other spiritual works God has done in their lives. It is a feeling of uncertainty and mistrust.

FACTS ABOUT DOUBT:

Doubt is a feeling, but we are not saved by feelings. We are saved by faith. Satan can tamper with your feelings, but he cannot void the work of God in your life. Determine that you will serve God even if you never "feel" anything that confirms your spiritual experience. Your eternal relationship with God is not based on feelings.

Doubt often results from disappointed with God. Perhaps He did not answer a prayer as you desired, or you feel He did not intervene in your circumstances as you had hoped.

Faith is the opposite of doubt. Faith is belief or trust in someone or something without overt proof. Biblically, faith is *"being sure of what we hope for and certain of what we do not see" (Hebrews 11:1)*. The basic tenets of our faith are the Word of God and the Gospel of the Lord Jesus Christ.

You are mandated to have faith in God. Jesus commanded: *"Have faith in God" (Mark 11:22)*. It is impossible to please God without faith. You must not only believe in God, but you must believe that He acts in your behalf: *"And without faith it is impossible to please God, because anyone who comes to him must believe that he exists and that he rewards those who earnestly seek him" (Hebrews 11:6)*.

You can be assured of your salvation because God's Word assures it (John 3:16; Romans 10:9; 1 John 1:9). You can be assured that:
> -Jesus paid your sin debt and obtained your full pardon: Colossians 2:13-14.
> -Your pardon is based on God's grace, which always exceeds your transgressions: Ephesians 1:7; Romans 5:20.
> -God does not hold your past or present sins against you as long as you have asked forgiveness: Romans 8:1; 2 Corinthians 5:19.
> -Forgiveness is extended to all who believe in Jesus: Acts 10:43.
> -Forgiveness is extended to believers who sin: John 1:9.

Assurance that eliminates doubt is not a matter of applying human logic. It is a matter of faith. You simply believe God's Word and do not rely on your own thinking (Proverbs 3:5).

DEALING WITH DOUBT:

Confess your sins to God: Sin can cause a lack of assurance about your spiritual status in God. Confess your sins regularly by using the model prayer for daily prayer (1 John 1:9 Proverbs 28:13).

Confess your doubts to God. *"...for what is not of faith is sin" (Romans 14:23).* Lack of faith shows you do not believe God at His Word. As the father who brought his ailing child to Jesus, cry out by faith, *"Lord I believe. Help me overcome my unbelief!" (Mark 9:24).*

Study the Word of God consistently.   The better you come to know God through His Word, the more you will trust Him completely with your salvation and in other spiritual issues (Romans 10:17; John 7:17; 1 John 5:13). Faith--the remedy for doubt--is increased through hearing, reading, and studying God's Word (Romans 10:17).

Refuse to allow the spirit of unbelief to operate in your life. In the first temptation, Satan caused Eve to doubt the Word of God.   Doubt is a tool of the enemy, so when Satan returns with doubtful thoughts, rebuke him, rebuke the thoughts, and cast them out in the name of Jesus.

WHAT GOD'S WORD SAYS ABOUT DOUBT:

The fool says in his heart, "There is no God." (Psalm 14:1)

Your word, O Lord, is eternal; it stands firm in the heavens. (Psalm 119:89)

Trust in the Lord with all your heart and lean not on your own understanding; in all your ways acknowledge him, and he will make your paths straight.   (Proverbs 3:5-6)

Then Jesus said to the centurion, "Go! It will be done just as you believed it would." (Matthew 8:13)

...your faith has healed you. (Matthew 9:22)

According to your faith will it be done to you... (Matthew 9:29)

Now He did not do many mighty works there because of their unbelief. (Matthews 13:58)

Immediately Jesus reached out his hand and caught him. "You of little faith," he said, "why did you doubt?"   (Matthew 14:31)

Then the disciples came to Jesus privately and said, "Why could we not cast it out?" So Jesus said to them, "Because of your unbelief; for assuredly, I say to you, if you have faith as a mustard seed, you will say to this mountain, 'Move from here to there,' and it will move; and nothing will be impossible for you." (Matthew 17:19-21, NKJV)

I tell you the truth, if you have faith and do not doubt, not only can you do what was done to the fig tree, but also you can say to this mountain, "Go, throw yourself into the sea," and it will be done. (Matthew 21:21)

He said to his disciples, "Why are you so afraid? Do you still have no faith?" (Mark 4:40)

He said to her, "Daughter, your faith has healed you. Go in peace and be freed from your suffering." (Mark 5:34)

Ignoring what they said, Jesus told the synagogue ruler, "Don't be afraid; just believe."
(Mark 5:36)

"Lord I believe. Help me overcome my unbelief!" (Mark 9:24).

"Go," said Jesus, "your faith has healed you." Immediately he received his sight and followed
Jesus along the road. (Mark 10:52)

"Where is your faith?" he asked his disciples. (Luke 8:22)

The apostles said to the Lord, "Increase our faith!" (Luke 17:5)

"Have faith in God," Jesus answered. "I tell you the truth, if anyone says to this mountain, 'Go,
throw yourself into the sea,' and does not doubt in his heart but believes that what he says will
happen, it will be done for him. Therefore, I tell you, whatever you ask for in prayer, believe
that you have received it, and it will be yours." (Mark 11:22-24)

Later He appeared to the eleven as they sat at the table; and He rebuked their unbelief and
hardness of heart, because they did not believe those who had seen Him after He had risen.
(Mark 15:14, NKJV)

Whoever believes and is baptized will be saved, but whoever does not believe will be
condemned. (Mark 16:16)

The disciples went and woke him, saying, "Master, Master, we're going to drown!" He got up
and rebuked the wind and the raging waters; the storm subsided, and all was calm. "Where is
your faith?" he asked his disciples. (Luke 8:24-25)

If you have faith as small as a mustard seed, you can say to this mulberry tree, "Be uprooted and
planted in the sea," and it will obey you. (Luke 17:6)

Yet to all who received him, to those who believed in his name, he gave the right to become
children of God-- children born not of natural descent, nor of human decision or a husband's will,
but born of God. (John 1:12-13)

For God so loved the world that he gave his one and only Son, that whoever believes in him shall
not perish but have eternal life. For God did not send his Son into the world to condemn the
world, but to save the world through him. (John 3:16)

Most assuredly, I say to you, he who hears My word and believes in Him who sent Me has
everlasting life, and shall not come into judgment, but has passed from death into life.
(John 5:24)

I tell you the truth, he who believes has everlasting life. (John 6:47)

I told you that you would die in your sins; if you do not believe that I am [the one I claim to be],
you will indeed die in your sins. (John 8:24)

My sheep listen to my voice; I know them, and they follow me. I give them eternal life, and they shall never perish; no one can snatch them out of my hand. My Father, who has given them to me, is greater than all; no one can snatch them out of my Father's hand. (John 10:27-28)

Even after Jesus had done all these miraculous signs in their presence, they still would not believe in him. (John 12:37)

Remain in me, and I will remain in you. (John 15:4)

Now Thomas (called Didymus), one of the Twelve, was not with the disciples when Jesus came. So the other disciples told him, "We have seen the Lord!" But he said to them, "Unless I see the nail marks in his hands and put my finger where the nails were, and put my hand into his side, I will not believe it." A week later his disciples were in the house again, and Thomas was with them. Though the doors were locked, Jesus came and stood among them and said, "Peace be with you!" Then he said to Thomas, "Put your finger here; see my hands. Reach out your hand and put it into my side. Stop doubting and believe." Thomas said to him, "My Lord and my God!" Then Jesus told him, "Because you have seen me, you have believed; blessed are those who have not seen and yet have believed." Jesus did many other miraculous signs in the presence of his disciples, which are not recorded in this book. But these are written that you may believe that Jesus is the Christ, the Son of God, and that by believing you may have life in his name. (John 20:24-31)

No, in all these things we are more than conquerors through him who loved us. For I am convinced that neither death nor life, neither angels nor demons, neither the present nor the future, nor any powers, neither height nor depth, nor anything else in all creation, will be able to separate us from the love of God that is in Christ Jesus our Lord. (Romans 8:37-39)

But what does it say? "The word is near you; it is in your mouth and in your heart," that is, the word of faith we are proclaiming: That if you confess with your mouth, "Jesus is Lord," and believe in your heart that God raised him from the dead, you will be saved. For it is with your heart that you believe and are justified, and it is with your mouth that you confess and are saved" (Romans 10:8-10).

...for, "Everyone who calls on the name of the Lord will be saved.   (Romans 10:13)

Consequently, faith comes from hearing the message, and the message is heard through the word of Christ. (Romans 10:17)

Be on your guard; stand firm in the faith; be men of courage; be strong. (1 Corinthians 16:13)

Now it is God who makes both us and you stand firm in Christ. He anointed us, set his seal of ownership on us, and put his Spirit in our hearts as a deposit, guaranteeing what is to come. (2 Corinthians 1:21-22)

...for by faith you stand. (2 Corinthians 1:24)

For it is by grace you have been saved, through faith--and this not from yourselves, it is the gift of God--not by works, so that no one can boast. (Ephesians 2:8-9)

In addition to all this, take up the shield of faith, with which you can extinguish all the flaming arrows of the evil one. (Ephesians 6:16)

..being confident of this, that he who began a good work in you will carry it on to completion until the day of Christ Jesus. (Philippians 1:6)

If we are faithless, he will remain faithful, for he cannot disown himself. (2 Timothy 2:13)

 I will therefore that men pray everywhere, lifting up holy hands, without wrath and doubting. (1 Timothy 2:8, KJV)

See to it, brothers, that none of you has a sinful, unbelieving heart that turns away from the living God. But encourage one another daily, as long as it is called Today, so that none of you may be hardened by sin's deceitfulness. (Hebrews 3:12-13)

So, do not throw away your confidence; it will be richly rewarded. You need to persevere so that when you have done the will of God, you will receive what he has promised. For in just a very little while, "He who is coming will come and will not delay. But my righteous one will live by faith. And if he shrinks back, I will not be pleased with him."   But we are not of those who shrink back and are destroyed, but of those who believe and are saved. (Hebrews 10:35)

Now faith is the assurance, the confirmation, the title deed of the things we hope for, being the proof of things we do not see, and the conviction of their reality. Faith is perceiving as real what is not revealed to the senses. (Hebrews 11:1, AMP)

And without faith it is impossible to please God, because anyone who comes to him must believe that he exists and that he rewards those who earnestly seek him. (Hebrews 11:6)

If any of you lacks wisdom, he should ask God, who gives generously to all without finding fault, and it will be given to him. But when he asks, he must believe and not doubt, because he who doubts is like a wave of the sea, blown and tossed by the wind. That man should not think he will receive anything from the Lord; he is a double-minded man, unstable in all he does. (James 1:5-8)

And God, in his mighty power, will protect you until you receive this salvation, because you are trusting him. It will be revealed on the last day for all to see. (1 Peter 1:5, NLT)

See that what you have heard from the beginning remains in you. If it does, you also will remain in the Son and in the Father.   And this is what he promised us--even eternal life. (1 John 2:24-25)

And now, dear children, continue in him, so that when he appears we may be confident and unashamed before him at his coming. (1 John 2:28)

I write these things to you who believe in the name of the Son of God so that you may know that you have eternal life. (1 John 5:13)

But you, dear friends, build yourselves up in your most holy faith and pray in the Holy Spirit (Jude 20)

But the cowardly, the unbelieving, the vile, the murderers, the sexually immoral, those who practice magic arts, the idolaters and all liars--their place will be in the fiery lake of burning sulfur. This is the second death." (Revelation 21:8)

CHAPTER SEVEN

The "it" of Oppression

DEFINITION: Oppression is a feeling of being heavily burdened, mentally or physically, by troubles, adverse conditions, anxiety, etc.

FACTS ABOUT OPPRESSION:

Oppression is not the same as possession by evil spirits. Oppression is a spiritual attack from the outside rather than inward possession by demonic powers. Oppression is usually caused by an attack of Satan upon your mind with fear, doubt, worry, torment, etc., that results in a heaviness of spirit--almost like a cloud that surrounds you. A believer can be oppressed, but not possessed because the Holy Spirit cannot abide in the same vessel with a demon.

Oppression can include physical conditions. Read the story of the woman who was oppressed with a physical condition for years and was healed by Jesus (Luke 13:10-11). This woman was not possessed, rather she was oppressed by a demonically-caused physical condition.

How oppressing spirits gain access. Evil spirits of oppression gain access through what you hear and see, through circumstances, and through negative influences by media or people around you.

Jesus came to deliver those oppressed by the devil. That includes you! The reason the Son of God appeared was to destroy the devil's work. (1 John 3:8)

God has given you power over oppression--not only over oppression, but overall the power of the enemy (Luke 10:19).

DEALING WITH OPPRESSION:

Recognize that oppression is Satanic. In Luke 13:10-17, the woman's condition was caused by oppression of the enemy. Satan also creates difficult circumstances which cause oppression. These can be easily recognized because they result in confusion--and God is not the author of confusion (1 Corinthians 14:33).

Recognize the signs of oppression. It may be a chronic sickness or a mental oppression that includes mental torment, confusion, doubt, restlessness, or an inability to reason. Emotional manifestations such as withdrawal and crying may also be present.

Determine how oppression is gaining access to your life. Satan causes oppression, but other sources contribute to it such as difficult circumstances and negative input from TV, Internet, music, and unwholesome literature. Deal with these issues and eliminate what is sinful.

Seek forgiveness for oppression that is the result of sin. Confess any sins that may have contributed to the oppression. For example, viewing pornography can result in shame and oppression by the enemy.

Pray a prayer of deliverance. Focus your prayer on the specific problems associated with your oppression. Go to the root cause: Satan and his demonic forces. Bind the spirits of oppression so that they are unable to operate.

Praise and worship the Lord. Satan hates praise and worship and the power of oppression will be broken in the presence of your sacrifice of praise (1 Samuel 16:23). Do it whether you feel like it or not. That is the meaning of a sacrifice of praise.

Eliminate practices that contribute to oppression. These include television programs, music, literature, and negative associates that are contributing to your oppression.

WHAT GOD'S WORD SAYS ABOUT OPPRESSION:

He went down with them and stood on a level place. A large crowd of his disciples was there and a great number of people from all over Judea, from Jerusalem, and from the coast of Tyre and Sidon, who had come to hear him and to be healed of their diseases. Those troubled by evil spirits were cured, (Luke 6:17-18)

Behold! I have given you authority and power to trample upon serpents and scorpions, and [physical and mental strength and ability] over all the power that the enemy [possesses]; and nothing shall in any way harm you. (Luke 10:19, AMP)

Read the story of the deliverance of the oppressed woman in Luke 13:10-16.

How God anointed and consecrated Jesus of Nazareth with the [Holy] Spirit and with strength and ability and power; how He went about doing good and, in particular, curing all who were harassed and oppressed by [the power of] the devil, for God was with Him. (Acts 10:38 AMP)

The reason the Son of God appeared was to destroy the devil's work. (1 John 3:8)

CHAPTER EIGHT

The "it" of Hopelessness

DEFINITION: Hope is an optimistic attitude of anticipation and confidence based on expectations of positive outcomes in the circumstances of one's life, the future, and the world at large. Hopelessness is the loss of hope.

FACTS ABOUT HOPELESSNESS:

The Bible is the ultimate source of eternal hope. *"For everything that was written in the past was written to teach us, so that through endurance and the encouragement of the Scriptures we might have hope" (Romans 15:4).*

What you think is a faith crisis may be a hope crisis. Hebrews 11:1 speaks of faith being the substance of hope. If you are hopeless, you have no substance for your faith and it is affected.

Some causes of hopelessness include associating with negative people, unanswered prayer, failure to control your thoughts, disappointment in other people, devastating circumstances, world conditions, and weariness from prolonged adversity.

How hope can be generated. Hope comes by making peace with God through Jesus, rejoicing in the hope of your eternal destination, and rejoicing despite sufferings: *"Therefore, since we have been justified through faith, we have peace with God through our Lord Jesus Christ, through whom we have gained access by faith into this grace in which we now stand. And we rejoice in the hope of the glory of God. Not only so, but we also rejoice in our sufferings, because we know that suffering produces perseverance; perseverance, character; and character, hope. And hope does not disappoint us, because God has poured out his love into our hearts by the Holy Spirit, whom he has given us" (Romans 5:1-5).*

Hope is an anchor for your spiritual experience. Hebrews 6:19 refers to hope as an "anchor of the soul". As an anchor prevents a boat from drifting off course, hope will do likewise for you spiritually. Hope continually pulls you back to the ways of God. Hope is related to your heart condition because "hope deferred makes the heart sick" (Proverbs 13:12). Hope is related to your joy, in that you rejoice in hope (Romans 12:12). Hope is also related to your salvation, as you are saved by hope (Romans 8:24).

DEALING WITH HOPELESSNESS:

Ask God to renew your hope. *"Be strong and take heart, all you who hope in the Lord" (Psalm 31:24).*

Put your hope in God instead of man. Very often, hopelessness results when you have been disappointed by trusting in man instead of God. The Psalmist said: *"Find rest, O my soul, in God alone; my hope comes from him" (Psalm 62:5).*

Spend time in God's Word. It is the source of eternal hope and your hope will be renewed as you study and practice its mandates. The Word of God was given so that we, through the scriptures, might have hope (Romans 15:4).

Choose hope-filled associates. Do not maintain close relationships with people who are negative, despondent, and hopeless. You learn the ways of those with whom you associate (Proverbs 22:24).

Control your mind. Negative, uncontrolled thoughts often lead to hopelessness. See the topic of "Mind And Thoughts" in this database.

Encourage yourself in the Lord as the psalmist did (1 Samuel 30:6). He said: *"Why are you downcast, O my soul? Why so disturbed within me? Put your hope in God, for I will yet praise him, my Savior and my God" (Psalm 42:5).*

Realize the purpose of tribulation is not to create hopelessness, rather it leads to developing hope: *"...we also rejoice in our sufferings, because we know that suffering produces perseverance; perseverance, character; and character, hope. And hope does not disappoint us, because God has poured out his love into our hearts by the Holy Spirit, whom he has given us" (Romans 5:3-5).*

Start a gratitude journal where you record what God is doing for you and the things for which you are grateful.   When you see how God is working in your life and all the things for which you can be thankful, your hope will be strengthened.

WHAT GOD'S WORD SAYS ABOUT HOPELESSNESS:

No one whose hope is in you will ever be put to shame. (Psalm 25:3)

You are God my Savior, and my hope is in you all day long. (Psalm 25:5)

Be strong and take heart, all you who hope in the Lord. (Psalm 31:24)

May your unfailing love rest upon us, O Lord, even as we put our hope in you. (Psalm 33:22)

Those who hope in the Lord will inherit the land. (Psalm 37:9)

For you have been my hope, O Sovereign Lord, my confidence since my youth. (Psalm 39:7)

Why are you downcast, O my soul? Why so disturbed within me? Put your hope in God, for I will yet praise him, my Savior and my God. (Psalm 42:5)

In your name I will hope, for your name is good. (Psalm 52:9)

Find rest, O my soul, in God alone; my hope comes from him. (Psalm 62:5)

But now, Lord, what do I look for? My hope is in you. (Psalms 71:5)

But as for me, I will always have hope; I will praise you more and more. (Psalm 71:14)

I have put my hope in your word. (Psalm 119:74)

Sustain me according to your promise, and I will live; do not let my hopes be dashed. (Psalm 119:116)

My soul faints with longing for your salvation, but I have put my hope in your word. (Psalm 119:81)

Hope deferred makes the heart sick, but a longing fulfilled is a tree of life. (Proverbs 13:12).

Yet this I call to mind and therefore I have hope: Because of the Lord's great love we are not consumed, for his compassions never fail. They are new every morning; great is your faithfulness. I say to myself, "The Lord is my portion; therefore, I will wait for him." The Lord is good to those whose hope is in him, to the one who seeks him. (Lamentations 3:21-25);

Therefore, since we have been justified through faith, we have peace with God through our Lord Jesus Christ, through whom we have gained access by faith into this grace in which we now stand. And we rejoice in the hope of the glory of God. Not only so, but we also rejoice in our sufferings, because we know that suffering produces perseverance; perseverance, character; and character, hope. And hope does not disappoint us, because God has poured out his love into our hearts by the Holy Spirit, whom he has given us. (Romans 5:1-5)

But hope that is seen is no hope at all. Who hopes for what he already has? But if we hope for what we do not yet have, we wait for it patiently. (Romans 8:24-25)

Be joyful in hope, patient in affliction, faithful in prayer. (Romans 12:12)

For everything that was written in the past was written to teach us, so that through endurance and the encouragement of the Scriptures we might have hope. (Romans 15:4)

May the God of hope fill you with all joy and peace as you trust in him, so that you may overflow with hope by the power of the Holy Spirit. (Romans 15:13)

Therefore, since we have such a hope, we are very bold. (2 Corinthians 3:12)

I pray also that the eyes of your heart may be enlightened in order that you may know the hope to which he has called you, the riches of his glorious inheritance in the saints, and his incomparably great power for us who believe. (Ephesians 1:18-19)

Remember that at that time you were separate from Christ, excluded from citizenship in Israel and foreigners to the covenants of the promise, without hope and without God in the world. But now in Christ Jesus you who once were far away have been brought near through the blood of Christ. (Ephesians 2:12-13)

There is one body and one Spirit--just as you were called to one hope when you were called--one Lord, one faith, one baptism; one God and Father of all, who is over all and through all and in all. (Ephesians 4:4-6)

Once you were alienated from God and were enemies in your minds because of your evil behavior. But now he has reconciled you by Christ's physical body through death to present you holy in his sight, without blemish and free from accusation--if you continue in your faith, established and firm, not moved from the hope held out in the gospel. (Colossians 1:21-23)

Brothers, we do not want you to be ignorant about those who fall asleep, or to grieve like the rest of men, who have no hope. We believe that Jesus died and rose again and so we believe that God will bring with Jesus those who have fallen asleep in him. (1 Thessalonians 4:13-15)

May our Lord Jesus Christ himself and God our Father, who loved us and by his grace gave us eternal encouragement and good hope, encourage your hearts and strengthen you in every good deed and word. (1 Thessalonians 2:16-17)

For the grace of God that brings salvation has appeared to all men. It teaches us to say "No" to ungodliness and worldly passions, and to live self-controlled, upright and godly lives in this present age, while we wait for the blessed hope--the glorious appearing of our great God and Savior, Jesus Christ, who gave himself for us to redeem us from all wickedness and to purify for himself a people that are his very own, eager to do what is good. (Titus 2:11-14)

... so that, having been justified by his grace, we might become heirs having the hope of eternal life. (Titus 3:7)

We have this hope as an anchor for the soul, firm and secure. (Hebrews 6:19)

Now faith is the assurance (the confirmation, the title deed) of the things [we] hope for, being the proof of things [we] do not see and the conviction of their reality [faith perceiving as real fact what is not revealed to the senses]. (Hebrews 11:1, AMP)

Praise be to the God and Father of our Lord Jesus Christ! In his great mercy he has given us new birth into a living hope through the resurrection of Jesus Christ form the dead.
(1 Peter 1:3)

Praise be to the God and Father of our Lord Jesus Christ! In his great mercy he has given us new birth into a living hope through the resurrection of Jesus Christ from the dead, and into an inheritance that can never perish, spoil or fade--kept in heaven for you, who through faith are shielded by God's power until the coming of the salvation that is ready to be revealed in the last time. (1 Peter 1:3-5)

Therefore, prepare your minds for action; be self-controlled; set your hope fully on the grace to be given you when Jesus Christ is revealed. (1 Peter 1:13)

Always be prepared to give an answer to everyone who asks you to give the reason for the hope that you have. But do this with gentleness and respect, keeping a clear conscience, so that those who speak maliciously against your good behavior in Christ may be ashamed of their slander. (1 Peter 3:15-16)

Everyone who has this hope in him purifies himself, just as he is pure. (1 John 3:3)

CHAPTER NINE

The "it" of Stress

DEFINITION: Stress is a physical, mental, or emotional response that causes physical, mental, or emotional tension.

FACTS ABOUT STRESS:

Stress can be internal, resulting from an illness, a medical procedure, and negative emotions like fear, anxiety, and worry. Unconfessed sin can cause spiritual stress.

Stress can be external, resulting from the environment or social situations.

Stress can result from both positive and negative circumstances. Things like a geographical relocation, a new job, a new baby--though positive experiences, may also be stressful. Negative circumstances such as a prolonged illness, the death of a loved one, a poor working or living situation may also cause stress.

Stress is related to other conditions including depression, high blood pressure, unresolved anger, etc.

Stress results from a lack of trust in God. If you trusted really Him to take care of your circumstances, you would not be stressed out about them.

DEALING WITH STRESS:

Analyze why you are stressed. Like David, question yourself: *"Why are you downcast, O my soul? Why so disturbed within me?"* Then, whatever the reason for your concern, tell yourself by faith: *"Put your hope in God, for I will yet praise him, my Savior and my God. My soul is downcast within me; therefore, I will remember you ..." (Psalm 42:5-6)*

Boldly declare that the Lord will help in any situation causing stress. He is your source of strength (Philippians 4:13). *"So, we take comfort and are encouraged and confidently and boldly say, The Lord is my helper, I will not be seized with alarm-I will not fear or dread or be terrified. What can man do to me?" (Heb. 13:6, TAB).*

Cast your cares on God. The Bible says to cast your cares on the Lord (Psalm 55:22). The word "cast" implies a continuous action. You may cast your cares on God, yet stressful thoughts return. When they do, cast again!

Pray instead of thinking about stressful circumstances. The Word says: *"Do not be anxious about anything, but in everything, by prayer and petition, with thanksgiving, present your requests to God. And the peace of God, which transcends all understanding, will guard your hearts and your minds in Christ Jesus" (Philippians 4:6-7).* Turn every stressful thought into a prayer.

Praise and worship God. It is impossible to remain stressed when you give yourself wholly to praise and worship. Put on some meditative Christian music and give it a try!

Take practical actions. If there is something you can change that will alleviate the stress, do so. For example, perhaps you could trim some of your commitments or seek a job change.

Replace stress with the Word. The Word of God is effective in dealing with stress. Following are some excerpts to get you started. In addition, go through your Bible and mark all of the promises of God and His faithfulness. Review these when you feel stressed.

WHAT GOD'S WORD SAYS ABOUT STRESS:

Commit your way to the Lord, Trust also in Him, And He shall bring it to pass. (Psalm 37:5, NKJV)

Do not fret--it leads only to evil. (Psalm 37:8)

I have been young, and now am old; Yet I have not seen the righteous forsaken, nor his descendants begging bread. (Psalm 37:25, NKJV)

Why are you downcast, O my soul? Why so disturbed within me? Put your hope in God, for I will yet praise him, my Savior and my God. My soul is downcast within me; therefore, I will remember you ... (Psalm 42:5-6)

Cast your cares on the Lord and he will sustain you; he will never let the righteous fall. (Psalm 55:22)

Praise the Lord, O my soul; all my inmost being, praise his holy name. Praise the Lord, O my soul, and forget not all his benefits--who forgives all your sins and heals all your diseases, who redeems your life from the pit and crowns you with love and compassion, who satisfies your desires with good things so that your youth is renewed like the eagle's. (Psalm 103:1-5)

When anxiety was great within me, your consolation brought joy to my soul. (Psalm 94:19)

An anxious heart weighs a man down, but a kind word cheers him up. (Proverbs 12:25)

The wicked man flees though no one pursues, but the righteous are as bold as a lion. (Proverbs 28:1)

Even youths grow tired and weary, and young men stumble and fall; but those who hope in the Lord will renew their strength. They will soar on wings like eagles; they will run and not grow weary, they will walk and not be faint. (Isaiah 40:30-31)
And why do you worry about clothes? See how the lilies of the field grow. They do not labor or spin. Yet I tell you that not even Solomon in all his splendor was dressed like one of these. If that is how God clothes the grass of the field, which is here today and tomorrow is thrown into the fire, will he not much more clothe you, O you of little faith? So, do not worry, saying, 'What

shall we eat?' or 'What shall we drink?' or 'What shall we wear?' For the pagans run after all these things, and your heavenly Father knows that you need them. But seek first his kingdom and his righteousness, and all these things will be given to you as well. Therefore, do not worry about tomorrow, for tomorrow will worry about itself. Each day has enough trouble of its own. (Matthew 6:28-34)

"Come to me, all you who are weary and burdened, and I will give you rest. Take my yoke upon you and learn from me, for I am gentle and humble in heart, and you will find rest for your souls. For my yoke is easy and my burden is light." (Matthews 11:28-30)

Therefore, I tell you, do not worry about your life, what you will eat; or about your body, what you will wear. Life is more than food and the body more than clothes. (Luke 12:22-23)

Be careful, or your hearts will be weighed down with dissipation, drunkenness and the anxieties of life, and that day will close on you unexpectedly like a trap. (Luke 21:34)

Peace I leave with you; my peace I give you. I do not give to you as the world gives. Do not let your hearts be troubled and do not be afraid. (John 14:27)

Do not be anxious about anything, but in everything, by prayer and petition, with thanksgiving, present your requests to God. And the peace of God, which transcends all understanding, will guard your hearts and your minds in Christ Jesus. (Philippians 4:6-7)

Cast all your anxiety on him because he cares for you. (1 Peter 5:7)

CHAPTER TEN

The "it" of Loneliness

DEFINITION: Loneliness is a sense of separation from people, often accompanied by isolation, depression, and feelings of rejection and self-pity. It is a lack of meaningful relationships with others.

FACTS ABOUT LONELINESS:

Loneliness is not the same as being alone. A person can be alone, and yet not be lonely. Conversely, one can be with many people and still feel lonely.

God never intended for you to live disconnected from others. One of the first things God did was establish a relationship with Adam and then provide him with a wife. God said it was not good to live in isolation (Genesis 2:18). God's plan was for you to have a meaningful relationship with Him and others.

Alienation was a result of the fall. When Adam and Eve sinned, they were alienated from God and began having problems in their relationship--blaming one another. All broken relationships are rooted in sin.

Intimacy with God is necessary in order to develop proper relationships with others. You will never be able to develop positive horizontal relationships with others until your vertical relationship with God is right. The only time Jesus expressed loneliness was when He was on the cross, alienated from the Father because He was bearing the sins of the world (Matthew 27:46).

Loneliness can be self-inflicted. If you do not try to make friends, you won't have any: *"A man who has friends must himself be friendly..."(Proverbs 18:24)* .

You are never really alone. Jesus promised to be with you always and He sent the Holy Spirit to be with you and dwell within you (John 14:17).

DEALING WITH LONELINESS:

Determine the cause for your loneliness. Deal with the root cause. Are you isolating yourself from others? Do you harbor unforgiveness? Are you staying too busy and disconnected from people? Have difficult circumstances--such as a tragedy or death--caused you to withdraw from others? Are you depressed?

Pray about your loneliness. Bind the spirits of isolation and self-pity that develop through loneliness. Release the comfort of the Holy Spirit who lives within you to operate in your life.

Restore broken relationships. If your loneliness is because of alienation from someone, seek to restore the relationship through forgiving and seeking forgiveness.

Develop godly friendships. Foster positive relationships with other believers. Do not be unevenly yoked in a friendship with an unbeliever (2 Corinthians 6:14).

Get involved with the Body of Christ. Join a church, attend a Bible study, or become part of a prayer group. Many friendships are formed through association with others in the Church. Start a special interest group in your church and recruit others who enjoy doing what you like to do.

Serve others. Squash self-pity and isolation by serving others. Volunteer at a homeless shelter or a food kitchen. Visit the elderly and shut-ins. Tutor a child. Volunteer for missions, prison ministry, or for service in your church. The opportunities are endless, and as you put yourself out there to serve, you will develop positive relationships with others.

Learn how to be a true friend. The biblical emphasis on relationships is evident when we note the number of times the words "one another" occurs, particularly in Paul's letters. We are commanded to:

-love one another: John 13:35
-be devoted to one another: Romans 12:10
-honor one another: Romans 12:10
-live in harmony with one another: Romans 12:16
-comfort one another: 1 Thessalonians 4:18
-encourage one another: Hebrews 3:13
-stir up one another to love and good works: Hebrews 10:24
-show hospitality to one another: 1 Peter 4:9
-employ the gifts of God for the benefit of one another: 1 Peter 4:10
-clothe yourself with humility towards one another: 1 Peter 5:5
-pray for one another: James 5:16
-confess your faults to one another; James 5:16
-speak to one another with psalms, hymns and spiritual songs: Ephesians 5:19
-submit to one another: Ephesians 5:21, 1 Peter 5:5
-consider others better than yourself: Philippians 2:3
-be concerned about the interests of others: Philippians 2:4
-bear with one another: Colossians 3:13
-teach one another: Colossians 3:16
-build up one another: Romans 14:19; 1 Thessalonians 5:11
-be likeminded towards one another: Romans 15:5
-accept one another unconditionally: Romans 15:7
-admonish one another: Romans 15:14; Colossians 3:16
-care for one another: 1 Corinthians 12:25
-serve one another: Galatians 5:13
-bear one another's burdens: Galatians 6:2
-forgive one another: Ephesians 4:2, 32; Colossians 3:13
-be patient with one another: Ephesians 4:2; Colossians 3:13
-be kind and compassionate to one another: Ephesians 4:32

WHAT GOD'S WORD SAYS ABOUT LONELINESS:

"Be strong and courageous. Do not be afraid or terrified because of them, for the Lord your God goes with you; he will never leave you nor forsake you." (Deuteronomy 31:6)

Though my father and mother forsake me, the Lord will receive me. (Psalm 27:10)

A man who has friends must himself be friendly... (Proverbs 18:24).

So, do not fear, for I am with you; do not be dismayed, for I am your God. I will strengthen you and help you; I will uphold you with my righteous right hand. (Isaiah 41:10)

"Though the mountains be shaken and the hills be removed, yet my unfailing love for you will not be shaken nor my covenant of peace be removed," says the Lord, who has compassion on you. (Isaiah 54:10)

And I will ask the Father, and he will give you another Counselor to be with you forever--the Spirit of truth. The world cannot accept him, because it neither sees him nor knows him. But you know him, for he lives with you and will be in you. I will not leave you as orphans; I will come to you. (John 14:16-18)

Who shall separate us from the love of Christ? Shall trouble or hardship or persecution or famine or nakedness or danger or sword? (Romans 8:35)

For I am convinced that neither death nor life, neither angels nor demons, neither the present nor the future, nor any powers, neither height nor depth, nor anything else in all creation, will be able to separate us from the love of God that is in Christ Jesus our Lord. (Romans 8:38-39)

God has said, "Never will I leave you; never will I forsake you." (Hebrews 13:5)

See also Psalm 139. You were never alone--not even in your mother's womb!

CHAPTER ELEVEN

The "it" of Suffering
(Adversities, Disasters and Tragedies)

DEFINITION: Suffering is pain that is experienced physically, mentally, or emotionally. It is distress that results from physical affliction, psychological and emotional troubles, loss, adversities, and tragedies.

FACTS ABOUT SUFFERING:

Suffering entered the world because of sin. From the time of the first sin committed by Adam and Eve in the Garden of Eden (Genesis 3:17-18), evil entered the world and suffering has been part of its tragic manifestations.

Suffering is not always due to personal sin. While it is true that you can suffer from the consequences of personal sin, all suffering is not caused by personal sin. That is one of the key revelations of the book of Job.

The ways suffering comes into the life of a believer include the following:

-*Persecution:* Some suffering comes through persecution because of a person's faith in God or their ministry. Saul pursued David because of his calling as king (1 Samuel 23). Haman attempted to annihilate the Jewish race (Esther 3:5-6). Daniel and his three friends suffered for their faith (Daniel 3:6). The Apostle Paul suffered intensely during his ministry (2 Corinthians 11:23-28). History records that many of the disciples of Christ died as martyrs.

-*Consequences:* Some suffering comes through consequences of not listening to good advice or rejecting the Word of the Lord. An analogy of this is found in the parable of the foolish man who built his house on sand and then had it collapse in the storm (Matthew 7:26-27). A modern-day example would be building your house in a known flood zone and suffering flooding because of your poor decision.

-*Others:* Sometimes you suffer because of those around you who create circumstances that cause difficulties for you. The relationship between Abraham and Lot is a good example. Abraham was constantly having problems because of Lot's poor decisions (Genesis 12-14).

-*Judgment:* God judges personal sin. Cain suffered for the murder of his brother Abel (Genesis 4:13-14). Joab was executed for killing two innocent men (1 Kings 2:32). God judged Adoni-Bezek for his inhumane treatment of enemy kings (Judges 1:7).

-*Discipline:* The purpose of discipline is to correct sin and restore a believer to right relationship with God. Nathan confronting David's sin and its subsequent judgment caused him to repent of adultery and murder (2 Samuel 11-12; Psalm 51).

-Ministry: Adversity prepares you to fulfill God's purposes and sometimes results from your ministry. Joseph suffered as a slave and a prisoner in order that the entire world could be saved from a great famine (Genesis 50:20). Jesus suffered and died so that the world could be saved from sin. The disciples were persecuted, imprisoned, and martyred for their ministries.

-Circumstances of life: Natural circumstances of life like tornados, floods, earthquakes, hurricanes, etc., can cause undeserved suffering.

-Satanic attack: Job chapters 1-2 illustrate how Satanic attack can be a cause of undeserved suffering.

Three important things to remember about suffering.
-There is a spiritual reason behind the suffering of the righteous: Job 1:6-12; 2: 1-6.
-Satan cannot afflict a believer without the permission of God: Job 1:6-12; 2: 1-6.
-God knows how much you can bear and will not let Satan go beyond this point: 1 Corinthians 10: 13.

Suffering takes many forms. It includes physical pain and the grief and sorrow caused by losses in life. Mental suffering can be caused by negative emotions like guilt, shame, remorse, anger, and unforgiveness. Suffering can also be manifested through depression and oppression caused by the enemy.

The normal responses to suffering include grief and sorrow which are intense emotional reactions to tragedy, suffering, and bereavement.

The call of Jesus to His followers was one of denial and suffering. See Matthew 10:38; 16:24; Mark 8:34; 10:21; Luke 9:23; 14:27 In each of these verses, Jesus calls His followers to deny themselves, take up their cross of suffering, and follow Him.

Suffering always has divine purpose. *"Wherein ye greatly rejoice, though now for a season, if need be, ye are in heaviness through manifold temptations: That the trial of your faith, being much more precious than of gold that perisheth, though it be tried with fire, might be found unto praise and honour and glory at the appearing of Jesus Christ" (1 Peter 1:6-7).* You learn that testing strengthens your character (James 1:2-3) and refines positive qualities in your life (Job 23:10). The writer of Hebrews says that trials and chastening prove that you are God's child (Hebrews 12:6-8).

Here are some positive benefits of suffering.

Your faith is tested: Everything in the spiritual world is based on faith. This is why the strength of your faith must be tested through trials (1 Peter 1:7).

You are able to comfort others: When you are comforted during trials, you learn how to extend that same comfort to others. (2 Corinthians 1:3-4).

You learn not to trust your own self: Paul spoke of the purpose of his sufferings in Asia, explaining that through them he learned not to trust in himself (2 Corinthians 1:8-9).

Positive qualities are developed: Qualities that conform you into the image of Christ are developed through suffering (1 Peter 5:10, Romans 8:28-29; Hebrews 2:10,18).

The works of God are manifested: When the disciples saw a man who had been blind from birth, they asked who was responsible for his condition. Was it the sin of his parents or those of the man himself? Jesus said that the man was suffering so that the works of God could be manifested in him (John 9:3).

The power of God is perfected: God's power is perfect despite your weaknesses (2 Corinthians 12:9).

That which is unstable is removed: Suffering results in all that is unstable being shaken out of your life. You cease to depend on people, programs, or material things because these all fail in your time of need (Hebrews 12:26-27). During the storms of life, everything crumbles that is not built upon God and His Word (Psalm 119:89 and Matthew 7:24-27).

Your focus is changed: When you experience suffering, you often focus your attention on cause and effect. You are concerned with what caused the difficult circumstances and the terrible effect it is having in your life. In suffering, God changes your focus from the temporal to the eternal (2 Corinthians 4:17-18; 1 Peter 4:12-13; 2 Timothy 2:12).

God prepares you for ministry: You want to be used by God, you desire to be more like Jesus, and to be a chosen vessel for His use. God answers your prayer through suffering because He chooses His ministers in the furnace of affliction (Isaiah 48:10).

You are prepared to reign with Christ: The Bible says if you suffer with Him, you will also reign with Him (2 Timothy 2:12).

You receive spiritual blessings: Jesus said your reward will be great in Heaven (Matthew 5:10-12).

You learn obedience: Even Jesus, who was sinless, learned obedience through suffering (Hebrews 5:8). Even a person who is righteous, good, and moral can learn more about obedience by suffering.

You are humbled: The Bible says that the nation of Israel was humbled because of the suffering experienced in the wilderness (Deuteronomy 8:15-16).

You come to know God more intimately: Job, who suffered much, learned this truth and declared that because of his suffering, he really came to see God in a new way (Job 42:5-6).

The important thing is to realize is that regardless of the reason for suffering, God is sovereign over it. Nothing happens of which He is not aware. He is merciful, ready to forgive and restore, and will help you through corrective, punitive, and undeserved suffering. Every day of your life was written before you were even born. No difficulty, suffering, or tragedy comes as a surprise to God (Psalm 139:13-18).

DEALING WITH SUFFERING:

Do not focus on reasons for your suffering. This was the original sin--wanting to know. Eve wanted to become as God and know all things (Genesis 3). For some tragedies, there are no good answers. The reason for some things will be revealed, others will not. You must learn that the secret things belong to the Lord (Deuteronomy 29:29). Commit your suffering and your unanswered questions to God.

Realize that Jesus bore your suffering. The Bible says Jesus was not only familiar--acquainted with grief--but that He also bore your grief and sorrow (Isaiah 53:3-5). Jesus bore your sin so that you no longer have to bear it. If He also bore your grief and sorrow, so why are you bearing it?

Release your feelings to God. Tell the Lord how you feel. Release your sorrow, grief, and questions to Him. If you are angry about your suffering, confess it to God. Ask God to heal your emotions. Know that the feelings you are experiencing are common in times of suffering but you do not have to continue having these feelings. God is able and ready to heal them.

Call upon the Holy Spirit to comfort you. One of the purposes of the Holy Spirit is to comfort in times of suffering, grief, and sorrow. When you are overwhelmed with suffering, call upon the Holy Spirit to come and fulfill His purpose of supernatural comfort (John 14:6). As a believer, you have the Comforter resident within you. He is always available in times of need. You are never alone. The Lord is near those whose hearts are broken (Psalm 34:18).

Focus on eternal things. If you focus on eternal things, your suffering actually works in your behalf (2 Corinthians 4:16-18). Do not focus on the circumstances of your suffering. Focus on God, His Word, His promises to you, and what He is doing in your life.

Know that all things are working together for your good. God takes all things--even the bad things, the losses, and sorrows--and weaves them together for good in the fabric of your life (Romans 8:28).

Remember these six "p"s of suffering:
-Purpose: God has divine purpose in your suffering.
-Profitable: Your suffering is profitable if you submit to God and trust Him.
-Presence: God is with you in your suffering.
-Prove: Your faith will be proven by the difficulties.
-Produce: Your suffering will produce positive spiritual qualities in your life.
-Perspective: You will emerge with a new perspective.

WHAT GOD'S WORD SAYS ABOUT SUFFERING:

The secret things belong to the Lord our God, but the things revealed belong to us and to our children forever... (Deuteronomy 29:29)

But he knows the way that I take; when he has tested me, I will come forth as gold. (Job 23:10)

Have no fear of sudden disaster or of the ruin that overtakes the wicked, for the Lord will be your confidence and will keep your foot from being snared. (Proverbs 3:25)

When calamity comes, the wicked are brought down, but even in death the righteous have a refuge. (Proverbs 14:32)

You hear, O Lord, the desire of the afflicted; you encourage them, and you listen to their cry. (Psalm 10:17)

He brought me out into a spacious place; he rescued me because he delighted in me. (Psalm 18:19)

For he has not despised or disdained the suffering of the afflicted one; he has not hidden his face from him but has listened to his cry for help. (Psalm 22:24)

Look upon my affliction and my distress and take away all my sins. (Psalm 25:18)

You turned my wailing into dancing; you removed my sackcloth and clothed me with joy, that my heart may sing to you and not be silent. (Psalm 30:11-12)

I will be glad and rejoice in your love, for you saw my affliction and knew the anguish of my soul. (Psalm 31:7)

Be merciful to me, O Lord, for I am in distress; my eyes grow weak with sorrow, my soul and my body with grief. (Psalm 31:9)

The Lord is close to the brokenhearted and saves those who are crushed in spirit. A righteous man may have many troubles, but the Lord delivers him from them all; (Psalm 34:18-19)

Why are you downcast, 0 my soul? Why so disturbed within me? Put your hope in God, for I will yet praise him, my Savior and my God. (Psalm 43:5)

For he has delivered me from all my troubles. (Psalm 54:7)

In God I trust; I will not be afraid. (Psalm 56:4)

I will take refuge in the shadow of your wings until the disaster has passed. (Psalm 57:1)

In my anguish I cried to the Lord, and he answered by setting me free. (Psalm 118:5)

My soul is weary with sorrow; strengthen me according to your word. (Psalm 119:28)

My comfort in my suffering is this: Your promise preserves my life. (Psalm 119:50)

Before I was afflicted I went astray, but now I obey your word. (Psalm 119:67)

It was good for me to be afflicted so that I might learn your decrees. (Psalm 119:71-72)

Preserve my life, O Lord, according to your word. (Psalm 119:107)

Look upon my suffering and deliver me, for I have not forgotten your law. (Psalm 119:153)

I call on the Lord in my distress, and he answers me. (Psalm 120:1)

The Lord will keep you from all harm--he will watch over your life; the Lord will watch over your coming and going both now and forevermore. (Psalm 121:7-8)

Though I walk in the midst of trouble, you preserve my life; you stretch out your hand against the anger of my foes, with your right hand you save me. (Psalm 138:7)

He heals the brokenhearted and binds up their wounds. (Psalm 147:3)

If you falter in times of trouble, how small is your strength! (Proverbs 24:10)

The Sovereign Lord will wipe away the tears from all faces. (Isaiah 25:8)

Surely it was for my benefit that I suffered such anguish. (Isaiah 38:17)

When you pass through the waters, I will be with you; And through the rivers, they shall not overflow you. When you walk through the fire, you shall not be burned, Nor shall the flame scorch you. (Isaiah 43:2)

I have tested you in the furnace of affliction. (Isaiah 48:10)

He is despised and rejected by men, A Man of sorrows and acquainted with grief. And we hid, as it were, our faces from Him; He was despised, and we did not esteem Him. Surely, He has borne our griefs and carried our sorrows; Yet we esteemed Him stricken, Smitten by God, and afflicted. But He was wounded for our transgressions, He was bruised for our iniquities;
The chastisement for our peace was upon Him, And by His stripes we are healed. (Isaiah 53:3-5)

Then you will call, and the Lord will answer; you will cry for help, and he will say: Here am I. (Isaiah 58:9)

Blessed are those who are persecuted because of righteousness, for theirs is the kingdom of heaven. (Matthew 5:10)

But before all these things, they will lay their hands on you and persecute you, delivering you up to the synagogues and prisons. You will be brought before kings and rulers for My name's sake. But it will turn out for you as an occasion for testimony.   Therefore, settle it in your hearts not to meditate beforehand on what you will answer; for I will give you a mouth and wisdom which all your adversaries will not be able to contradict or resist. (Luke 21:12, NKJV)

And I will ask the Father, and he will give you another Counselor to be with you forever. (John 14:16)

But the Counselor, the Holy Spirit, whom the Father will send in my name, will teach you all things and will remind you of everything I have said to you. Peace I leave with you; my peace I give you. I do not give to you as the world gives. Do not let your hearts be troubled and do not be afraid. (John 14:26-27)

Remember the words I spoke to you: 'No servant is greater than his master.' If they persecuted me, they will persecute you also. If they obeyed my teaching, they will obey yours also. They will treat you this way because of my name, for they do not know the One who sent me (John 15:20-21)

I tell you the truth, you will weep and mourn while the world rejoices. You will grieve, but your grief will turn to joy. (John 16:20)

"These things I have spoken to you, that in Me you may have peace. In the world you will have tribulation; but be of good cheer, I have overcome the world." (John 16:33)

And when they had preached the gospel to that city, and had taught many, they returned again to Lystra, and to Iconium, and Antioch, Confirming the souls of the disciples, and exhorting them to continue in the faith, and that we must through much tribulation enter into the kingdom of God. (Acts 14:20-22, KJV)

I only know that in every city the Holy Spirit warns me that prison and hardships are facing me. However, I consider my life worth nothing to me, if only I may finish the race and complete the task the Lord Jesus has given me--the task of testifying to the gospel of God's grace. (Acts 20:23)

Not only so, but we also rejoice in our sufferings, because we know that suffering produces perseverance; perseverance, character; and character, hope. And hope does not disappoint us, because God has poured out his love into our hearts by the Holy Spirit, whom he has given us. (Romans 5:3-5)

I consider that our present sufferings are not worth comparing with the glory that will be joy revealed in us. (Romans 8:18)

And we know that in all things God works for the good of those who love him, who have been called according to his purpose. (Romans 8:28)

Who shall separate us from the love of Christ? Shall trouble or hardship or persecution or famine or nakedness or danger or sword? As it is written: "For your sake we face death all day long; we are considered as sheep to be slaughtered."   No, in all these things we are more than conquerors through him who loved us. For I am convinced that neither death nor life, neither angels nor demons, neither the present nor the future, nor any powers, neither height nor depth, nor anything else in all creation, will be able to separate us from the love of God that is in Christ Jesus our Lord. (Romans 8:35-38)

Be joyful in hope, patient in affliction, faithful in prayer. (Romans 12:13)

We work hard with our own hands. When we are cursed, we bless; when we are persecuted, we endure it; when we are slandered, we answer kindly. Up to this moment we have become the scum of the earth, the refuse of the world. (1 Corinthians 4:12-13)

For just as the sufferings of Christ flow over into our lives, so also through Christ our comfort overflows. If we are distressed, it is for your comfort and salvation; if we are comforted, it is for your comfort, which produces in you patient endurance of the same sufferings we suffer. And our hope for you is firm, because we know that just as you share in our sufferings, so also you share in our comfort. (2 Corinthians 1:5-7)

But we have this treasure in jars of clay to show that this all-surpassing power is from God and not from us. We are hard pressed on every side, but not crushed; perplexed, but not in despair; persecuted, but not abandoned; struck down, but not destroyed. (2 Corinthians 4:7-9)

Therefore, we do not lose heart. Though outwardly we are wasting away, yet inwardly we are being renewed day by day. For our light and momentary troubles are achieving for us an eternal glory that far outweighs them all. So, we fix our eyes not on what is seen, but on what is unseen. For what is seen is temporary, but what is unseen is eternal. (2 Corinthians 4:16-18)

If the earthly tent we live in is destroyed, we have a building from God, an eternal house in heaven, not built by human hands. (2 Corinthians 5:1)

Rather, as servants of God we commend ourselves in every way: in great endurance; in troubles, hardships and distresses; in beatings, imprisonments and riots; in hard work, sleepless nights and hunger; in purity, understanding, patience and kindness; in the Holy Spirit and in sincere love; in truthful speech and in the power of God; with weapons of righteousness in the right hand and in the left; through glory and dishonor, bad report and good report; genuine, yet regarded as impostors; known, yet regarded as unknown; dying, and yet we live on; beaten, and yet not killed; sorrowful, yet always rejoicing; poor, yet making many rich; having nothing, and yet possessing everything. (2 Corinthians 6:4-10)

For it has been granted to you on behalf of Christ not only to believe on him, but also to suffer for him, (Philippians 1:29)

But whatever was to my profit I now consider loss for the sake of Christ. What is more, I consider everything a loss compared to the surpassing greatness of knowing Christ Jesus my

Lord, for whose sake I have lost all things. I consider them rubbish, that I may gain Christ and be found in him, not having a righteousness of my own that comes from the law, but that which is through faith in Christ--the righteousness that comes from God and is by faith. I want to know Christ and the power of his resurrection and the fellowship of sharing in his sufferings, becoming like him in his death, and so, somehow, to attain to the resurrection from the dead.
(Philippians 3:7-11)

...so that no one would be unsettled by these trials. You know quite well that we were destined for them. In fact, when we were with you, we kept telling you that we would be persecuted. And it turned out that way, as you well know. (1 Thessalonians 3:3-4)

Therefore, among God's churches we boast about your perseverance and faith in all the persecutions and trials you are enduring. All this is evidence that God's judgment is right, and as a result you will be counted worthy of the kingdom of God, for which you are suffering. God is just: He will pay back trouble to those who trouble you and give relief to you who are troubled, and to us as well. This will happen when the Lord Jesus is revealed from heaven in blazing fire with his powerful angels. (2 Thessalonians 1:4-5)

Thou therefore endure hardness, as a good soldier of Jesus Christ. (2 Timothy 2:3)

Yea, and all that will live godly in Christ Jesus shall suffer persecution. (2 Timothy 3:12)

But you be watchful in all things, endure afflictions, do the work of an evangelist, fulfill your ministry. (2 Timothy 4:5, NKJV)

Remember those earlier days after you had received the light, when you stood your ground in a great contest in the face of suffering. Sometimes you were publicly exposed to insult and persecution; at other times you stood side by side with those who were so treated. You sympathized with those in prison and joyfully accepted the confiscation of your property, because you knew that you yourselves had better and lasting possessions. So do not throw away your confidence; it will be richly rewarded. You need to persevere so that when you have done the will of God, you will receive what he has promised. For in just a very little while,
He who is coming will come and will not delay. But my righteous one will live by faith.
And if he shrinks back, I will not be pleased with him. But we are not of those who shrink back and are destroyed, but of those who believe and are saved. (Hebrews 10:32-39)

Hebrews chapter 11: The hall of fame for faithful men and women of God who suffered.

Endure hardship as discipline; God is treating you as sons. For what son is not disciplined by his father? If you are not disciplined (and everyone undergoes discipline), then you are illegitimate children and not true sons. Moreover, we have all had human fathers who disciplined us and we respected them for it. How much more should we submit to the Father of our spirits and live! Our fathers disciplined us for a little while as they thought best; but God disciplines us for our good, that we may share in his holiness. No discipline seems pleasant at the time, but painful. Later on, however, it produces a harvest of righteousness and peace for those who have been trained by it. (Hebrews 12:7-11)

Consider it pure joy, my brothers, whenever you face trials of many kinds, because you know that the testing of your faith develops perseverance. Perseverance must finish its work so that you may be mature and complete, not lacking anything. (James 1:2-4)

Blessed is the man who perseveres under trial, because when he has stood the test, he will receive the crown of life that God has promised to those who love him. (James 1:12)

Brothers, as an example of patience in the face of suffering, take the prophets who spoke in the name of the Lord. As you know, we consider blessed those who have persevered. You have heard of Job's perseverance and have seen what the Lord finally brought about. The Lord is full of compassion and mercy. (James 5:10-11)

In this you greatly rejoice, though now for a little while you may have had to suffer grief in all kinds of trials. These have come so that your faith--of greater worth than gold, which perishes even though refined by fire--may be proved genuine and may result in praise, glory and honor when Jesus Christ is revealed. (1 Peter 1:6-7)

For it is commendable if a man bears up under the pain of unjust suffering because he is conscious of God. But how is it to your credit if you receive a beating for doing wrong and endure it? But if you suffer for doing good and you endure it, this is commendable before God. To this you were called, because Christ suffered for you, leaving you an example, that you should follow in his steps. (1 Peter 2:19-22)

Therefore, since Christ suffered in his body, arm yourselves also with the same attitude, because he who has suffered in his body is done with sin. (1 Peter 4:1)

Dear friends, do not be surprised at the painful trial you are suffering, as though something strange were happening to you. But rejoice that you participate in the sufferings of Christ, so that you may be overjoyed when his glory is revealed. If you are insulted because of the name of Christ, you are blessed, for the Spirit of glory and of God rests on you. If you suffer, it should not be as a murderer or thief or any other kind of criminal, or even as a meddler. However, if you suffer as a Christian, do not be ashamed, but praise God that you bear that name. (1 Peter 4:12-14)

So then, those who suffer according to God's will should commit themselves to their faithful Creator and continue to do good. (1 Peter 4:19)

And the God of all grace, who called you to his eternal glory in Christ, after you have suffered a little while, will himself restore you and make you strong, firm and steadfast. (1 Peter 5:10)

And I heard a loud voice from the throne saying, "Now the dwelling of God is with men, and he will live with them. They will be his people, and God himself will be with them and be their God. He will wipe every tear from their eyes. There will be no more death or mourning or crying or pain, for the old order of things has passed away." (Revelation 21:3-4)

CHAPTER TWELVE

The "it" of Suicide

DEFINITION: Suicide is when a person chooses to end their own life and deliberately kills themselves. Assisted suicide is when you help someone commit suicide.

(Note: If you are ministering in a telephone counseling center and someone calls who is threatening suicide, a life depends on your actions. First, get their name and location. Keep them on the line while another person dials to dispatch emergency response personal to their location. The person calling for emergency assistance should relay the exact location and the nature of the emergency--suicide in progress, threats of suicide, etc. Keep the caller talking with you, listening and encouraging them. Do not panic. Take control, believing that the Holy Spirit will speak through you. Tell the caller that you will remain on the line until the emergency workers arrive at the location. The primary objective is to prevent the suicide. Prayer and biblical counseling can follow. The type of counseling that asks "What do you think you should do about this problem" is not appropriate. You already know what they think. They believe the answer is death! Take authority on the basis of the Word of God and show them suicide is not the answer, but that God has an answer. Minister hope for the future.)

FACTS ABOUT SUICIDE:

Suicide destroys, so we know the thought of it and acting upon are not from God. John 10:10 confirms that it is the enemy who kills, steals, and destroys.

People consider suicide when their problems or sins seem greater than their coping mechanisms. That is why salvation through the blood of Jesus is so important. He forgives and bears your sin, grief, and pain so that you no longer have to cope with these feelings alone

Suicide attempts are usually a result of emotional issues. A great loss or tragedy can trigger suicidal thoughts--death of a loved one, loss of a business, finances, or a significant relationship, and chronic health problems are examples. Depression and unstable mental conditions also result in suicidal thoughts or attempts. Anger at others can cause thoughts of suicide to "show them" and make those who have wronged them feel guilty.

How does someone get to the point of suicide? Everyone goes through periods in their lives when they feel down. In time, the feelings usually depart and life goes on. But sometimes, difficult situations lead to feelings of depression, guilt, shame, and unhappiness that do not go away. Life becomes a great struggle filled with gloom, despair, emptiness, and hopelessness. Eventually, a person feels there is nothing to live for and seeks a way out of his pain.

Assisted suicide is sometimes requested by people who want to die because of a devastating illness. They ask someone to help them or a doctor to provide lethal medications. Some governments have made laws against this, while others endorse it as a way to "die with dignity". This practice is also called "euthanasia". But it is God who gives life (Job 33:4) and He who has numbered our days (Job 14:5). Hebrews 9:27 indicates that the time of one's death is appointed.

65

When you decide to end your own life for any reason, you are arrogantly saying you know better than God.   There is nothing in the Bible that says we have to keep someone alive for as long as possible, however. If someone is terminally ill and in great pain, they should be made as comfortable as possible and comforted by the Word of God and prayer. The same God that sustained you in life, will sustain you in death.   (Note: Having an order of "do not resuscitate-- DNR" is not suicide or assisted suicide, nor is disconnecting life support when someone has been declared brain dead. In cases of terminal illness, mental disorders, and advanced age, such orders are merely expressing a desire for doctors not to intervene in the natural process of dying or to be kept alive artificially. God is greater than any DNR order or any disconnect of life support systems. He can still intervene and supernaturally restore life.

Suicide is the ultimate act of selfishness. The person committing suicide is thinking only of himself and what he perceives to be an end to his problems. He does not think about the mental and emotional pain and possible financial hardships he will cause in the lives of friends and relatives who are left behind. Suicide is a waste of the gift of life that God intended be used for His glory. It is a frightening finality that results from unresolved hopelessness, despair, and tragedy.

Attempted suicide is a cry for help. Suicide is an act taken by one who actually wants to die, but futile attempts at it are cries for help. Take them seriously.

Suicide is not a problem of a specific class of people. Educated and uneducated, rich and poor, young and old--all are affected by it. The tendency towards suicide cannot be inherited and does not run in families. It can, however, be a learned behavior, i.e., a person considers it because their parent dealt with their problems by ending it all.

Symptoms of suicide can include hinting about it, making a threat, actual attempts, and not rebounding properly after a significant loss or tragedy. Isolation, abandoning previous interests, and giving away cherished possessions are also signs. Increase in drug and alcohol use, depression, and hopelessness are other symptoms that a person is considering suicide. Sometimes, however, a person who has been extremely depressed seems to be happier than they have been for some time. Often, this is mistaken as a sign that the person is getting better and no longer suicidal. In truth, their seeming happiness is resulting from having made a decision to commit suicide and knowing there will be an end to their problems.

Suicide is murder, and murder is sin. It is spiritually and morally wrong for a person to rebelliously decide they have the right to end their own life by murdering themselves. Your body is the temple of the Holy Spirit and you must respect that (1 Corinthians 6:19). Assisted suicide--where you help someone commit this act--is also sin. You are aiding in the death of a human being, and according to the Bible murder is sin. In many nations, the law views this as a crime and there will be legal ramifications.

Suicide is not an unpardonable sin. Just as murder can be forgiven, suicide is not the unpardonable sin. God is merciful and He knows our weaknesses. If a believer had just told a lie and then dropped dead, would he be eternally lost? No. Thus, God's grace can forgive suicide by a professing believer--someone who loses hope and in a moment of anguish makes a terrible decision. There is nothing in the Bible that specifically addresses whether someone who commits suicide is eternally lost, but we know that salvation is not by works--it is by grace. And nothing can separate you from the love of God.

Believers are not immune from suicide. We live in a fallen world, and Christians suffer great losses and tragedies just as unbelievers do. Sometimes a believer may be so emotionally fragile that they cannot deal with their problems and they consider suicide as a way out. We cannot understand the depth of someone else's suffering or the tragic reasons that could drive someone to commit this act. Only God knows what is in a person's heart.

People sometimes refer to the Old Testament character, Samson, and claim that he committed suicide, but that is not true. Samson sacrificed his life to free his nation from a powerful and evil enemy. It would be similar to jumping in front of a speeding car to save the life of your child. That is sacrifice, not suicide (Judges 16). This is why Samson is listed as a hero in the Bible's record of faithful men and women (Hebrews 11:32). Suicides in the Bible were committed by sinful men acting in desperation and disgrace. They included Abimelech (Judges 9:54); Saul and his armor bearer (1 Samuel 31:3-6); Ahithophel (2 Samuel 17:23); Zimri (1 Kings 16:18); and Judas (Matthew 27:5).

DEALING WITH SUICIDE:

If you do not know God, become a believer. Although believers are sometime tempted with suicidal thoughts, most often a suicide spirit manifests itself in unbelievers. Becoming a believer in Jesus Christ will make you a new creature in Christ and give you hope for the future. As a child of God, you will have God working in your behalf in difficult times. If you have never made a decision to accept Jesus Christ as your personal Savior, you can do that right now and take the first step toward a new life. Simply pray this prayer and mean it in your heart: *"Lord Jesus, I ask you to come into my life. I want to turn from living my life under my own control. Come now and live your life in me. Jesus, forgive me for my sins. I receive you as my Lord and my Savior. I will live for you and serve you all the days of my life. Amen"*.

Determine what is causing thoughts of suicide. Is it a recent loss? Is it a health issue? Is it depression in general? Deal with the root causes in prayer. People often turn to suicide because they are seeking relief from pain. Jesus Christ bore your pain--as well as your sins--on the cross, so why are you bearing your own pain? Ask God to heal your pain. Do not minimize the issues that are causing your thoughts of suicide. Acknowledge and deal with them in the name of Jesus.

Share your feelings with your spiritual leader. Christian leaders can provide guidance, prayer, and encouragement through this difficult time.

Rebuke the spirit of suicide from operating. Suicide is a Satanic spirit that would take your life! Don't let it! Rebuke every thought of it in the name of Jesus.

Know that no matter how dark things seem at the time, there is hope in the future. Things will get better. You will come through this dark time of your life. God did not promise that you won't have problems, but He gives you the ability to face challenges through His supernatural power.

Formulate a plan for the future. With the help of a biblical counselor or Christian friend, make plans for the future. Your plan should include Bible study, prayer, and fellowship with other believers. It should also include steps to deal with issues that have contributed to the thoughts of suicide. A plan will give you hope for the future.

Read the following passages and make them your declarations of faith: Psalm 23; Psalm 28:7; Isaiah 43:2; Romans 8:28; and Philippians 4:13.

Start a gratitude journal. Each day, write down something for which you are grateful. This will keep you focused on the positive things in your life instead of the negative.

If you are a relative or friend of someone who has committed suicide, take solace in the Word of God, prayer, and comfort of Christian friends. Do not withdraw from others. Release your anger and disappointment at the person for this act, and believe that God was merciful to him/her in their desperate time of need.

WHAT GOD'S WORD SAYS ABOUT SUICIDE:

You shall not murder (Exodus 20:13)

This day I call heaven and earth as witnesses against you that I have set before you life and death, blessings and curses. Now choose life, so that you and your children may live and that you may love the Lord your God, listen to his voice, and hold fast to him. For the Lord is your life, and he will give you many years... (Deuteronomy 30:15)

I am still confident of this: I will see the goodness of the Lord in the land of the living. Wait for the Lord; be strong and take heart and wait for the Lord. (Psalm 27:13-14)

Read Psalm 73 where the Psalmist expressed his despair, but ends by expressing his trust in the Lord.

Though I walk in the midst of trouble, you preserve my life; you stretch out your hand against the anger of my foes, with your right hand you save me. The Lord will fulfill [his purpose] for me; your love, O Lord, endures forever--do not abandon the works of your hands. (Psalm 138:7-8)

"For I know the plans I have for you," declares the Lord, "plans to prosper you and not to harm you, plans to give you hope and a future." (Jeremiah 29:11)

Yet this I call to mind and therefore I have hope: Because of the Lord's great love we are not consumed, for his compassions never fail. They are new every morning; great is your

faithfulness. I say to myself, "The Lord is my portion; therefore, I will wait for him."
(Lamentations 3:21-24)

For I take no pleasure in the death of anyone, declares the Sovereign Lord. Repent and live!
(Ezekiel 18:32)

Then Jesus told his disciples a parable to show them that they should always pray and not give
up. (Luke 18:1)

The thief comes only to steal and kill and destroy; I have come that they may have life, and have
it to the full. (John 10:10)

For I am convinced that neither death nor life, neither angels nor demons, neither the present nor
the future, nor any powers, neither height nor depth, nor anything else in all creation, will be able
to separate us from the love of God that is in Christ Jesus our Lord. (Romans 8:38-39)

Do you not know that you are the temple of God and that the Spirit of God dwells in you? If
anyone defiles the temple of God, God will destroy him. For the temple of God is holy, which
temple you are. (1 Corinthians 3:16-17)

Or do you not know that your body is the temple of the Holy Spirit who is in you, whom you
have from God, and you are not your own? For you were bought at a price; therefore, glorify
God in your body and in your spirit, which are God's. (1 Corinthians 6:19-20)

But he said to me, "My grace is sufficient for you, for my power is made perfect in weakness."
Therefore, I will boast all the more gladly about my weaknesses, so that Christ's power may rest
on me. That is why, for Christ's sake, I delight in weaknesses, in insults, in hardships, in
persecutions, in difficulties. For when I am weak, then I am strong. (2 Corinthians 12:9-10)

Do not be anxious about anything, but in everything, by prayer and petition, with thanksgiving,
present your requests to God. And the peace of God, which transcends all understanding, will
guard your hearts and your minds in Christ Jesus. Finally, brothers, whatever is true, whatever is
noble, whatever is right, whatever is pure, whatever is lovely, whatever is admirable--if anything
is excellent or praiseworthy--think about such things. (Philippians 4:6-8)

So, do not throw away your confidence; it will be richly rewarded. You need to persevere so that
when you have done the will of God, you will receive what he has promised. (Hebrews 10:35-
36)

CONCLUSION

How to Get Rid of "it" though Personal Deliverance

When you understand self-deliverance, you will keep yourself from being bond; you will keep yourself healthy, physically and spiritually and be free from spiritual pollution. Every day, you will enjoy divine health and will not be spending your money on drugs and hospital bills.

Sometimes, there may not be a minister who is anointed and knowledgeable about deliverance to help you. Sometimes, you can be heavily attacked and the next service is about four days away. What do you do? You should never allow evil spirits to reside in your life. If you lack adequate time to do a self-deliverance in the mornings, after your quiet time, then, when you're having your bath, you could do it.

Whatever the causes of our spiritual afflictions, there are several proven steps we may try to help ourselves find freedom and healing. If these steps do not resolve your situation, then perhaps it is time to ask for help:

Step 1 — Conversion

Deliverance from any level of bondage, or harassment (collectively called, "spiritual afflictions") cannot be achieved without personal conversion. Deliverance from milder forms of spiritual affliction may often be achieved by the various acts of personal conversion—Acts of Contrition, Faith, Hope, Charity, and Consecration. "Prayer Acts" and other prayers, with fasting, and various devotions are often effective to drive evil spirits away:

So humble yourselves before God. Resist the Devil, and he will flee from you. Draw close to God, and God will draw close to you. — (James 4:7,8)

The first step, therefore, is make up your mind to live the Christ-life; or if already doing so, to persevere in living the Christ-life. This internal conversion, which is a conscious decision and determination to follow Christ and all of His teachings, precedes all other steps to deliverance. Without conversion to the Faith in Jesus Christ and participation in His family, the Church, deliverance, even if seemingly effective for a while, cannot be successful in the long run. It is the *"Truth"* that makes us free (John 8:31b), not prayers, rituals, counseling, or personal will in themselves. It is the confrontation with Truth that sends the demons running back to hell. This is why the method of Deliverance Counseling we use is called a *"Truth Encounter"*. As demons are confronted with the Truth, and as we are confronted with the Truth, of whom we are in Christ, we gain freedom. The foundation of all truth is Jesus Christ, who is Truth (John 14:6). Without our Lord Jesus Christ, we can never know truth or obtain it.

Some people believe they are unable to make a profession of faith in Jesus Christ. In such cases the person should ask God for help—ask Him for the faith that will save, deliver, and heal.

If we are willing to accept the gift of faith from God, our Lord will give it to us when we ask:

70

And I tell you, Ask, and it will be given you; seek, and you will find; knock, and it will be opened to you. For every one who asks receives, and he who seeks finds, and to him who knocks it will be opened. What father among you, if his son asks for a fish, will instead of a fish give him a serpent; or if he asks for an egg, will give him a scorpion? If you then, who are evil, know how to give good gifts to your children, how much more will the heavenly Father give the Holy Spirit to those who ask him! — (Luke 11:9-13)

Sincerely ask God for the faith that brings saving faith, the faith of conversion to the One, that is Jesus Christ, whom who declares:

I am the way, and the truth, and the life; no one comes to the Father, but by me (John 14:6) .... Come to me, all who labor and are heavy laden, and I will give you rest (Matthew 11:28) .... I will not reject anyone who comes to me (John 6:37) .... [rather] take my yoke upon you, and learn from me; for I am gentle and lowly in heart, and you will find rest for your souls. For my yoke is easy, and my burden is light (Matt 11:29-30)

Step 2 — Repentance

Essential to growing closer to God in faith, devotion, and love is to repent of those behaviors, desires, beliefs, and ideas that are sinful. The definition of sin is much broader than most people imagine. A definition of sin:

Sin is an offense against reason, truth, and right conscience; it is a failure in genuine love for God and neighbor caused by a perverse attachment to certain goods. Its wounds the nature of man and injures human solidarity. It has been defined as "an utterance, a deed, or a desire contrary to the eternal law."

Sin is an offense against God: *"Against you, you alone, have I sinned, and done that which is evil in your sight"* (Ps 51:4). Sin sets itself against God's love for us and turns our hearts away from it. Like the first sin (of Adam and Eve), it is disobedience, a revolt against God through the will to become "like gods" (Gen 3:5), knowing and determining good and evil. Sin is thus "love of oneself even to contempt of God." In this proud self-exaltation, sin is diametrically opposed to the obedience of Jesus, which achieves our salvation (cf. Phil 2:6-9).

We must repent of our sin, but repentance involves more than merely "turning away" from sin. Repentance must also renounce all that opposes God and all that He finds sinful. This includes renouncing Satan and his ways, renouncing personal sins, and renouncing all that leads us to sin. Some of the common sins and situations that interfere with deliverance include: involvement in non-Christian activities like the occult; persistent situational sins such as living together without marriage or remarriage without annulment of previous marriages; maintaining improper or problematic friendships; illegal activities of any sort; and sins that have become habitual such as pornography, masturbation, fornication, gossip, lying, stealing, etc.

The three greatest stumbling blocks to deliverance is Pride, Rebellion, and Unforgiveness and all the things that go along with those three sins. Repentance of Pride, Rebellion, and Unforgiveness is required to even hope for deliverance. Repentance also includes the firm amendment to avoid sin, and the near occasion of sin, in the future. Repentance requires a *complete* turnaround of our lives, a becoming a *"new man"*, so that...

...you should put away the old self of your former way of life, corrupted through deceitful desires, and be renewed in the spirit of your minds, and put on the new self, created in God's way in righteousness and holiness of truth. Therefore, putting away falsehood, speak the truth, each one to his neighbor, for we are members one of another...(thus) do not leave room for the devil (Eph 4:22-25,26b)

Step 3 — Confession

With faith and contrition of heart, repentance of mind, firm purpose to avoid sin and that which leads us to sin, we must now confess our sins before our God who is a God of forgiveness and mercy. This is a critical step that we will discuss at length.

The manner of our confession differs, but within our respective traditions, confession is required:

If we confess our sins, he is faithful and just, and will forgive our sins and cleanse us from all unrighteousness. (1 John 1:9)

... if you confess with your mouth that Jesus is Lord and believe in your heart that God raised him from the dead, you will be saved. For one believes with the heart and so is justified, and one confesses with the mouth and so is saved. (Romans 10:9-10)

"Confess your sins to each other and pray for each other so that you may be healed. The earnest prayer of a righteous person has great power and wonderful results" (James 5:16).

This confidant maybe one's pastor or another minister, or a trusted friend. We must be careful when choosing an "accountability partner." Since we will be revealing very private and sensitive information about ourselves, it is critically important to trust whoever we choose as a confidant to be discreet and to keep absolutely confidential the information we tell them.

There is wisdom in presenting oneself to an "accountability partner." Personal accountability is upheld when we confess to another person whom may hold us accountable for our actions. Confessing our sins to one another is a powerful way to break the bonds of sin in our lives. It is much harder to confess our sins to one another than to simply say, *"Lord, forgive me"*. While God is forgiving, of course, it is the demands of personal accountability before another human being that brings our confession into grounded reality that strengthens our commitment to turn away from sin in the future.

Religious ministers, psychologists, counselors, and others including the Deliverance Counselors of agency, are also bound either by law, ethical codes, or contract with the client (or bound by any combination thereof) to keep private and confidential all that is revealed to them. In addition, those in the ministerial and helping professions are usually trained in the ethics, legalities, and culture of maintaining confidentiality. They are use to keeping private the personal information of their patients and clients. Friends, on the other hand, may not have such training and may not be use to the culture of confidentiality. Thus, if one's confidant is not a pastor, or at least a minister, psychologist, or counselor bound by law and/or ethical codes, take care to ensure the chosen confidant understands thoroughly that he must keep private all that he hears and may not discuss it with anyone, not even with his spouse.

There is a great psychological comfort in hearing the words, "I forgive you" or the equivalent, "I absolve you of your sins." Our Father in heaven understands this psychological need. Thus, in His great love for us, He provided a way for us to hear those words in His name. It is God who ultimately forgives sins, but God, according to His sovereign authority chose to delegate this authority to His validly ordained priests. This power was given to the Apostles in John 20:22-23 and was passed on from them to those whom they appointed.

Our Father in heaven also knows and understands our need to be a family and for the family to come to our aid when we are hurting, to offer forgiveness when we fall, and to provide healing and strength to help us grow in faith. God forgives you when you appeal to Him with your heart-felt and sincere repentance and confession. Follow the tradition of your denomination and always offer a prayer for forgiveness as soon as possible after sinning. Then, in obedience to the Bible, seek accountability by confession to a confidant to complete your healing.

Step 4 — Removing the Greatest Stumbling blocks: Pride, Rebellion, and Forgiveness

We have already mentioned that the three biggest stumbling blocks to deliverance is usually Pride, Rebellion, and Unforgiveness. These three sins distance us from God. To draw closer to God we need to give up our pride, obey our Lord's teachings, and forgive those who hurt us.

In Deliverance Counseling we help our clients through exercises to locate pockets of pride and rebellion and to rid themselves of these sins with the help of God through prayer. Forgiveness, however, tends to be the most difficult, partly because of pride or even rebellion perhaps, but mostly because of deeply emotional issues surrounding the circumstances of the hurts someone has given us. Whatever the causes of our unforgiveness, deliverance is not possible until we can come to forgive, thus we shall discuss this topic at some length too.

The following guide is rather long, but this step is one of the most important. One simple MUST deals with Pride, Rebellion, and Unforgiveness if deliverance and healing is to be permanently possible.

Pride: Pride is the essential sin that leads to most other sins. It is the sin of Lucifer that led him to rebel against God resulting in his expulsion from heaven and becoming Satan.

Pride is a killer. Pride says, "I can do it! I can get myself out of this mess without God and without anyone else's helped." No, we can't! We absolutely need God, and we desperately need each other.

Pride also says "I know the best and most efficient way and how dare others get in the way of that" or "How dare things not go my way" or "How dare some person or something get in the way of what I want to do." Impatience is a factor of pride. Other ways impatience reveals our pride is getting impatient when we cannot find our car keys, or when we are late to a meeting, or if someone is driving too slowly for us on the hi-way, or when the computer acts up and interrupts our train of thought.

Impatience is the sister to Pride because it is caused essentially by our desire to have things our own way, in our own time, and according to our own preferences.

Pride is also the engine behind egotism (thinking more of oneself than one ought) and behind false humility (putting oneself down to be less than what one actually is). Pride is the force behind resistance to lawful and appropriate authority — whether that authority is a parent, teacher, police officer, government, employer, or the Church.

Pride is the basis of thinking of oneself as better than others, being pompous, and having contempt toward one's neighbors, employers, other family members, or the Church and her ministers.

Pride can also rear its ugly head in more subtle ways such as reluctance to apologize when we need to apologize, demanding our rights merely because it is our right, being inappropriately unkind or rude, jealousy, being quick-tempered, moodiness, brooding over wrongs done by others to oneself, depression and despair, or demanding that we are right about something, when indeed we are right about the issue, even though the issue is unimportant or can be handled differently (this is a major phenomenon in marriages, families, and friendships — the phrase "We need to choose our battles" is an important remedy for this).

Other ways that Pride expresses itself include: by taking personal credit for gifts or possessions and thus refusing to acknowledge that we have what we have by God's Providence; glorying in our achievements as if they were not primary a result of God's grace and divine goodness; by minimizing one's defeats; by claiming qualities that are not actually possessed; magnifying the faults and defects of others or dwelling upon the defects and faults of others.

James 4:6-10 and 1 Peter 5:1-10 reveals that spiritual conflict follows pride.

Examine yourself for these and any other attributes of pride and then pray:

Dear Heavenly Father. You have said that pride goes before destruction and an arrogant spirit before stumbling (Prov. 16:18). I confess that I have not denied myself, picked up my cross daily, and followed You (Matt. 16:24). In so doing I have given ground to the enemy in my life. I have believed that I could be successful and live victoriously by my own strength and resources. I now confess that I have sinned against You by placing my will before You and by centering my life around self instead of You.

I now renounce the self-life and by so doing cancel all the ground that has been gained in my life by the enemies of the Lord Jesus Christ. I pray that You will guide me so that I will do nothing from selfishness or empty conceit, but with humility of mind that I will regard others as more important than myself (Phil. 2:3). Enable me through love to serve others and in honor prefer others (Rom. 12:10). Amen.

Rebellion: We often place our confidence in the flesh not only with the "I can do it myself" attitude but each time we assert our own opinions above the teachings of Christ. It is a pride and a rebellion to say, "I want to do it my way" or "I want to think the way I want" without regard to the ways God teaches us to go and to believe. This is an arrogance that not only can get us into major trouble but also forms a major vulnerability for demons to come into our life.

Rebelling against God and His authority gives Satan an opportunity to attack. As our commanding general, the Lord Jesus Christ says, *"Get into ranks and follow Me. I will not lead you into temptation, but I will deliver you from evil."*

The Bible teaches us that it is the will of God for us to be obedient to parents, to civil government, to the Church, and to the pastors who are over us. We have two biblical responsibilities in regard to these authority figures: 1) Pray for them; and 2) submit to them. The only time God permits us to disobey those in authority over us is when they require of us an act or acquiescence in ways that are contrary to Church Law, Natural Law, or Divine Law.

Being under authority is an act of faith; we are trusting God to work through His established lines of authority. The authority that God has ordained does not mean, however, that we are to submit to abuse from those authorities. In those cases where someone in authority over us is abusing us in any way, then we need to act in appropriate ways according to the situation — such as appeal to the state for protection and relief for civil or criminal issues; or appeal to Church authorities on some issue involving religion or our parish; or make appropriate decisions such as terminating an abusive relationship, etc. Whoever the authority, who is abusing, we need to pray for the offender and to forgive him; but we are not required to be a doormat or target of their abuse.

Some of the lines of authority mentioned in the Bible include:

- Church leaders (Hebrews 13:17; Matthew 18:15-18)
- Parents (Ephesians 6: 1-3; Exodus 20:12)
- Husbands (1 Peter 3:1-3; Ephesians 5:23-24)
- Employers (1 Peter 2:18-21)
- Civil Government (Romans 13:1-5; 1 Timothy 2:1-3; 1 Peter 2:13-16)

Examine yourself for any areas of rebellion (deliberate driving faster than the speed limit is rebellion, too, you know!) and then pray:

Dear Heavenly Father. You have said that rebellion is as the sin of witchcraft and insubordination is as iniquity and idolatry (1 Sam. 15.23). I know that in action and attitude I have sinned against You with a rebellious heart. I ask Your forgiveness for my rebellion and pray that by the shed blood of the Lord Jesus Christ, strengthened by intercession of the that all ground gained by evil spirits because of my rebelliousness be canceled and taken back. I pray that You will shed light on all my ways that I may know the full extent of my rebelliousness, and I now choose to adopt a submissive spirit and a servant's heart. Amen.

Unforgiveness: Jesus Himself discusses the seriousness of failing to forgive. He tells us that failure to forgive those who hurt us will result in our not being forgiven ourselves by God. *"Forgive us our trespasses (sins) as we forgive those who trespass (sin) against us"*. The *Our Father*, the Lord's Prayer, which most all of us know and pray, Jesus teaches us that God will be as forgiving to us as we are to others.

Indeed, how can we expect God to forgive us when we do not forgive our brothers? Consider the follow teachings from Holy Scripture:

If you forgive those who sin against you, your heavenly Father will forgive you. But if you refuse to forgive others, your Father will not forgive your sins (Matthew 6:14,15).

But when you are praying, first forgive anyone you are holding a grudge against, so that your Father in heaven will forgive your sins, too (Mark 11:25).

If you forgive others, you will be forgiven. (Luke 6:37b)

Forgiveness is not about emotions and feelings. You can still be hurting, angry and upset and still decide to forgive. Forgiveness involves a mental decision, a decision of will, an act of your free will, even though you may not "Feel it".

The true nature of forgiveness:

1. **Forgiveness is not forgetting:** People who try to forget find that cannot. It is an unfortunate quirk of the English language with the phrase, "Forgive and forget". In actuality this phrase does not mean to "forget" in the sense of not remembering what happened; of course, we will remember. God says He will "remember our sins no more" (Heb. 10: 17), but God, being omniscient, obviously cannot literally forget. "Remember no more" means that God will never use the past against us (Ps. 103:12).

   To forget is really "to let go". We need to *"let go and let God"*. We let go of the past, but more importantly we let go of the hurt. As long as we do not forgive, as long as we do not let go, we allow the offender of our wounds continue to hurt us.

2. **Forgiveness is a choice not a feeling:** Since God requires us to forgive, <u>it is something we can do</u>. God will NEVER ask us to do something that is impossible for us to do; that would be cruel and God is a loving God.

   Forgiveness, however, is difficult for us because it pulls against our feelings and emotional hurts. Forgiveness is not about forgetting our feelings or our emotional hurts. We often will not "feel" like forgiving, but we must forgive anyway. As the Lord Prayer teaches us, God forgives us "as we forgive others". But how can God require this of us when we have been hurt so badly?

   God does not expect your feelings and emotional hurts to be healed overnight. He knows and understands our feelings and our hurts. He is a compassionate God and will help us to heal over time, as we are able. What God expects of us is not an immediate emotional healing, but a decision of will to forgive, a decision of will to trust Him to take care of the offender and to heal us, a decision of will to ask God for, and to commit to, being healed of our wounds.

3. **Forgiveness is not letting the person off the hook:** Forgiving is about you letting go, but it is not letting the offender off the hook. He will still pay for what he did, either before the Law or before God or both.

Forgiving is surely difficult for us because it pulls against our concept of justice. We want revenge for offenses suffered. But we are told never to take our own revenge (Rom. 12:9). Revenge does more damage to us than it punishes the offender. God's justice will prevail, no one can escape it. Never fear, those who hurt us will be held accountable, but we must let God deal with it. In order for God to deal with it, we need to let Him deal with it by letting go.

"Why should I let them off the hook?" But doing that is precisely the problem — we are still hooked to them, still bound by our past when we do not forgive.

To forgive does not mean letting the person off the hook; it means letting yourself off the hook.

4. **But you don't understand how much this person hurt me:** The problem is that when we do not forgive we, in essence, allow the person to still hurt us! The question is, "How do we stop the pain?" The answer is **to forgive!**

It is important to understand that we do not forgive someone for their sake; we do it for our sake so we can be free. Our need to forgive is not an issue between the offender and us; it is between us and God.

5. **Forgiveness is agreeing to live with the consequences of another's sin:** Forgiveness is costly. We pay the price of the evil we forgive. We are going to live with those consequences whether we want to or not; our only choice is whether or not we will do so in the slavery of bitterness and unforgiveness or with the freedom of forgiveness.

Jesus took the consequences of our sin upon Himself. All true forgiveness is substitution because no one really forgives without bearing the consequences of the other person's sin. God the Father *"made Him who knew no sin to be sin on our behalf, that we might become the righteousness of God in Him"* (2 Cor. 5:2 1).

Where is the justice? We might ask. It is the Cross that makes forgiveness legally and morally right: *"For the death that He died, He died to sin, once for all"* (Rom. 6: 10). This doesn't mean that we tolerate sin. We must always stand against sin, but we must give the offender to God and get on with our life.

6. **How do we forgive from our heart?** First, we acknowledge the hurt and the hate. If our forgiveness does not visit the emotional core of our life, it will be incomplete. Many feel the pain of interpersonal offenses, but they will not

acknowledge it. Let God bring the pain to the surface so He can deal with it. This is where the healing takes place.

Do not wait to forgive until we feel like forgiving; we will never get there. Feelings take time to heal mostly <u>after</u> the choice to forgive is made and Satan has lost his place (Eph. 4:26, 27). Freedom is what will be gained, not a feeling.

7. **Summary of Points on Forgiveness:**
   - Forgiveness is necessary to have fellowship with God.
   - It is not forgetting.
   - It is a choice.
   - Letting the offender off <u>our</u> hook is what frees us.
   - The offender is not off God's hook.
   - God says, "Revenge is mine."
   - You must acknowledge the hurt and the hate.
   - Forgiveness means we are agreeing to live with the consequences of another's sin — which we have to do anyway.
   - The justice is in the cross.
   - Choice is between the slavery of bitterness or the freedom of forgiveness.
   - Forgiveness means not using the past against the offender.
   - Forgiveness <u>does not</u> mean tolerating the sin or abuse.
   - Why forgive? To stop the pain! As we live in unforgiveness the offender still hurts us!
   - The issue of forgiveness is between you and God only.
   - The act of forgiveness is for your sake, and for your freedom.

Think about the people in your life for whom you need to forgive, people to whom you hold bitterness, people who have hurt you or disappointed you in anyway, or for whom you hold any kind of grudge. Be sure to ALWAYS include your parents, siblings, spouse, and YOURSELF. There is always something to forgive in our families and in ourselves.

Record all the names you can think of on a sheet of paper and a brief note as to why you need to forgive them. If you do not remember names, list them by what you do remember, such as "the guy in sixth grade with the red hat". If you cannot remember why you need to forgive someone on your list that is okay; forgive them for whatever it was — God knows.

After preparing this list ask God to bring to your mind anyone you have forgotten. It is not unusual to forget, or to push aside from our conscious mind, incidents and even the names of people whom have hurt us. These hidden hurts and wounds need to be healed as well. Thus, ask God to bring to your mind any person you have forgotten for whom you need to forgive, for whom you hold a grudge against, for which you are bitter, for those who have hurt you, with the following prayer:

Father in heaven, please bring to my mind the names of any people for whom I have held bitterness towards, grudges against, or have not forgiven for the hurts they have caused me. Help me to remember all these hurts so that they may be offered to You, O Lord, and healed from my soul so that I may live the truly victorious Christ-life. Amen.

Add to your list the names of anyone God may bring to your mind.

Now it is time to pray...

The following prayer needs to be said for each person on the list for which you need to forgive. Do not go to the next person on the list until you are sure you have dealt with all the remembered pain.

As you pray, God may bring to your mind various offending people and experiences that has been totally forgotten. Allow God to do this even if it is painful. Remember this process of forgiveness is for your sake because God wants you to be free.

Remember also that by forgiving the offender we are not rationalizing or trying to explain the offender's behavior. Forgiveness deals with the victim's pain, your pain, not another's excuses. Positive feelings will follow in time; freeing you from the past is the critical issue now.

If you are willing to forgive for your sake, so that you can walk away from this webpage free in Christ, free from the past and from person who hurt you, pray the introductory prayer below and then pray the "Prayer to Forgive" for each person on your list:

Heavenly Father, I now ask for your help in forgiving all those people on my list. Although I am still hurt and angry with them, I know that they are your children and that you love them more than I can possibly know. For this reason, my God, I ask you to help me forgive them. I lay down all bitterness, resentment and hatred for this person and I freely choose to forgive them. Teach me to be more merciful, my God, and help me be always willing, just as you are always willing, to forgive those who sin against me. Amen."

Prayer to Forgive

Lord, I forgive _________________________________ for (specifically identify all offenses and painful memories).

May God heal you and bless you!

Step 5 — Know Who You Are in Christ!

In order to gain freedom, it is important to know who you are in Christ. Thus, you need to evaluate the concept you have of yourself, to acknowledge the truth about God and about yourself; about your relationship and ideas about God and about the manner of our lives.

We often deceive ourselves about our position in Christ and our relationship with Him. For example, we may say to ourselves: "This isn't going to work" or "I wish I could believe this but I can't" or perhaps even more direct deceptions or denials concerning the promises of God for His children. Areas of deception that we may have include:

1. **Self-Deception** (telling ourselves things that are not true)

- Listening to God's words but thinking we do not have to do it (Ja 1:22; 4:17)
- Thinking we have no sin or do not sin (1 Jn 1:8)
- Thinking that we are something when we are not (Gal 6:3)
- Believing that we will not reap what we sow (Gal 6:7)
- Thinking we are wise and sophisticated in the 21st century (1 Cor 3:18, 19)
- Believing that the unrighteous will reach heaven (1 Cor 6:9)
- Thinking we can associate with bad company and not be corrupted (1 Cor 15:33)

2. **Self-Defense** (defending ourselves instead of trusting Christ)
    - Denial (conscious or subconscious)
    - Fantasy (escape from the real world)
    - Emotional insulation (withdraw to avoid rejection)
    - Regression (reverting back to a less threatening time in the past)
    - Displacement (taking out frustrations on others)
    - Projection (blaming others or accusing others of things we ourselves have done)
    - Rationalization (defending self though verbal excursion)

To counter these and other deceptions we tell ourselves we need to exercise faith. Faith is the response to Truth and believing the truth is a CHOICE (not a feeling). If we say, "I want to believe God, but I just can't," then we are deceiving ourselves. Of course, we can believe God. We know that God does not lie. Faith is something we DECIDE to do; it is not something we FEEL like doing. Believing the truth does not make it true; rather it is TRUE, therefore we believe it.

Examine yourself and how you may deceive yourself with "self-deceptions" and "Self-Defense" mechanisms. The pray the following prayer: ...

Prayer to Know the Truth:

Dear Heavenly Father. I know that You desire truth in the inner self and that facing this truth is the way of liberation (John 8:32). I acknowledge that I have been deceived by the father of lies (John 8:44) and that I have deceived myself (1 John 1:8). I pray in the name of the Lord Jesus Christ, and since by faith I have received You into my life and am now seated with Christ in the heavenliest (Eph 2:6), I ask you Father to command all deceiving spirits to depart from me. I now ask You to *"search me, O God, and know my heart: try me and know my anxious thoughts; and see if there be any hurtful way in me, and lead me in the everlasting way"* (Ps. 139:23, 24) In the name of Christ Jesus I pray. Amen.

Knowing the truth about oneself, overcoming self-deceptions and the mechanism of self-defense that hide who we really are, includes understanding our faith in Christ. It is by Christ that our lives have meaning and substance.

The following prayer is the substance of that faith:

Affirmations

I believe that I am a child of God (1 Jn. 3:1-3) and that I am seated with Christ in the heavenlies (Eph. 2:6). I believe that I was saved by the grace of God through faith that is a gift and not the result of my own efforts or merits (Eph 2:8).

I choose to be strong in the Lord and in the strength of His might (Eph 6:10). I put no confidence in the flesh (Phil 3:3) for the weapons of warfare are not of the flesh (2 Cor. 10:4). I put on the whole armor of God (Eph. 6:10-20), and I resolve to stand firm in my faith and to resist the evil one.

I believe that Jesus Christ has all authority in heaven and on earth (Matt 28:18) and that He is the head over all rule and authority (Col 2:10). I believe that Satan and his demons and wicked spirits are subject to the Lord Jesus Christ and therefore to me in Christ since I am a member of Christ's body (Eph 1:19-23).

I believe that apart from Christ I can do nothing (John 15:5) so I declare my dependence upon Him.

I choose to abide in Christ in order to bear much fruit and to glorify the Lord (Jn 15:8) and to accomplish the work of sanctification that Christ began in me through the Cross (James 2).

I believe that since I am a member go God's royal family I have the authority, in the name of Christ Jesus, to ask the Father to command the devil to leave my presence, as I obey the command to resist the devil (James 4:7).

I reject any counterfeit gifts or works of Satan and his minions in my life.

I believe that the truth will set me free (John 8:32) and that walking in the light is the only path of fellowship and freedom (1 John 1:7). Therefore, as a royal member of God's household, I stand against Satan's deceptions by affirming all the doctrines of the Faith and by taking every thought captive in obedience to Christ (2 Cor 10:5).

I declare that the Bible and the Church are the only authoritative standards for me (2 Tim 3:15, 16).

I choose to speak the truth in love (Eph 4:15).

I choose to present my body as an instrument of righteousness, a living and holy sacrifice, and thus I renew my mind daily by the living Word of God in order that I may prove that the will of God is good, acceptable, and perfect (Rom 6:13; 12:1, 2).

I ask my heavenly Father to fill me with His Holy Spirit (Eph 5:18), to lead me into all truth (John 16:13), and to empower my life that I may live above sin and not carry out the desires of the flesh (Gal 5:16). I crucify the flesh (Gal 5:24) and choose to walk by the Spirit.

In making all these affirmations, I renounce all selfish goals and choose the ultimate goal of love (1 Tim 1:5). I choose to obey the greatest commandment to love the Lord my God will all my heart, soul, and mind, and to love my neighbor as myself (Matt 22:37-39). Amen.

Step 6 — Worship, Pray, and Fast

Worship as a Church Family: One of Satan's favorite lies, apart from having us believe that he does not exist, or that he does exist and is more powerful than he truly is, is that since God is everywhere and we can worship Him anywhere and do not need the "community of believers ", the Church family.

Although it is true that God is everywhere and worshiping Him anywhere is wholesome and good, it is false to believe that the Church is unnecessary. Since the earliest days of Christianity, communities of believers gathered together on the *Lord's Day* (Sunday).

Scripture is very clear on the subject of Church attendance and on how our submission to its authority is not only good but required. The Church, its leaders and members, are the Mystical Body of Christ here on Earth. To disobey the teachings of the Church as it relates to faith and morals is to disobey the teachings of Christ. To not attend church is also disobedience to Christ.

Paul admonishes those who do not come to Church in Hebrews 10:19-25:

Therefore, brothers, since through the blood of Jesus we have confidence of entrance into the sanctuary by the new and living way he opened for us through the veil, that is, his flesh, and since we have "a great priest over the house of God," let us approach with a sincere heart and in absolute trust, with our hearts sprinkled clean from an evil conscience and our bodies washed in pure water. Let us hold unwaveringly to our confession that gives us hope, for he who made the promise is trustworthy. We must consider how to rouse one another to love and good works. We should not stay away from our assembly, as is the custom of some, but encourage one another, and this all the more as you see the day drawing near.

Hebrews 13:17

Obey your leaders and submit to them; for they are keeping watch over your souls, as men who will have to give account. Let them do this joyfully, and not sadly, for that would be of no advantage to you.

Worship and prayer together as a family, prayer meetings, adoration, and other corporate settings, and in the privacy of the family at home is critical in developing spiritual health for the family and each family member. Such family devotion forms the foundation for all that each family does away from home in the world of school, work, and society.

Prayer is so important both in the family context and individually. It is important not just because prayer is something a Christian ought to do, but because prayer is communication.

The more we depend on God, the closer He is to us and we are to Him. Aligning ourselves with God, communicating with Him at all times and in all situations and personal decisions will unite our hearts to His. A heart united to the Creator will overflow with graces and blessings.

Prayer and Spiritual Warfare: In addition, a healthy prayer life destroys strongholds that demons may have in our lives and in our hearts. Without prayer we cannot hope to be delivered from spiritual afflictions. It is no secret —prayer, worship, devotion, and living the Christ-Life in all that it entails is the formula not only for deliverance from spiritual afflictions, but for living the victorious life in Christ.

When dealing with spiritual afflictions, however, some special prayer considerations may be needed. Scripture states that there are certain demons that will only respond to prayer as well as fasting: *"But this kind does not go out except by prayer and fasting."* (Matthew 17:21). If fasting can defeat even the strongest of fallen angels, just how powerful is this sacrifice that we can make?

Spiritual warfare prayers are very effective in defeating the enemy and drawing our hearts closer to God.

Step 7 — Live the Faith and Remain Faithful

Along with all the advice and recommendations of the first six steps, our healing and deliverance cannot be complete unless we act upon our faith. Doing good works and charitable acts of love are a natural outflow of our faith and necessary to lead a good Christian life. It is not enough to believe. James asks and admonishes in James 2:19,20, 26:

Do you still think it's enough just to believe that there is one God? Well, even the demons believe this, and they tremble in terror! Fool! When will you ever learn that faith that does not result in good deeds is useless?

Just as the body is dead without a spirit, so also faith is dead without good deeds.

James calls a man a fool who does not act upon his faith in James 1:22-25:

Be doers of the word and not hearers only, deluding yourselves. For if anyone is a hearer of the Word and not a doer, he is like a man who looks at his own face in a mirror. He sees himself, then goes off and promptly forgets what he looks like. But the one who peers into the prefect law of freedom and perseveres, and is not a hearer who forgets but a doer who acts, such a one shall be blessed in what he does.

It is hard to live the Christ-Life, but we must try. We must not have a faith that is dead and useless. We must not be a fool and not practice our faith. We must, rather, live out our faith and persevere in the faith:

1 Corinthians 9:23-27

All this I do for the sake of the gospel, so that I too may have a share in it. Do you not know that the runners in the stadium all run in the race, but only one wins the prize? Run so as to win. Every athlete exercises discipline in every way. They do it to win a perishable crown, but we an imperishable one. Thus, I do not run aimlessly; I do not fight as if I were shadowboxing. No, I drive my body and train it, for fear that, after having preached to others, I myself should be disqualified.

Colossians 1:17-23

He is before all things, and in him all things hold together. He is the head of the body, the church. He is the beginning, the firstborn from the dead, that in all things he himself might be preeminent. For in him all the fullness was pleased to dwell, and through him to reconcile all things for him, making peace by the blood of his cross (through him), whether those on earth or those in heaven.

And you who once were alienated and hostile in mind because of evil deeds he has now reconciled in his fleshly body through his death, to present you holy, without blemish, and irreproachable before him, provided that you persevere in the faith, firmly grounded, stable, and not shifting from the hope of the gospel that you heard, which has been preached to every creature under heaven, of which I, Paul, am a minister.

And thus, let us be able to say, with St. Paul, in 2 Timothy 4:6-8

For I am already on the point of being sacrificed; the time of my departure has come. I have fought the good fight, I have finished the race, I have kept the faith. Henceforth there is laid up for me the crown of righteousness, which the Lord, the righteous judge, will award to me on that Day, and not only to me but also to all who have loved His appearing.

Persevere in the faith and let your life be a living Gospel for you shall thereby *"know the truth and the truth shall set you free"*

I have outlined steps detailing certain issues that we have found important in gaining freedom for a person in spiritual affliction.

1. purify one's conscience by a good confession;
2. Receive Holy Communion as often as possible;
3. Implore the mercy of God by prayer and fasting.
4. Recourse to specific spiritual warfare prayers applicable to the situation.

Final Thoughts

Repentance, forgiveness, acting on our faith, praying, fasting, receiving the Sacrament frequently, and all the rest we ought to do as good Christians are very good things and very necessary for this life, but more importantly for the life to come.

The advice contained in these Steps to Self-Deliverance, however, are not "quick fixes". This advice involves a lifelong commitment for anyone with spiritual afflictions. Freeing yourself from the bondages of the enemy and keeping them from returning requires this commitment to persevere in Christ and in the Christ-life.

There will be dry times. Your faith will be tested. Indeed, the demons may (and more than likely will) try to return. Scripture speaks of what demons do once they are cast out:

Now when the unclean spirit goes out of a man, it passes through waterless places seeking rest, and does not find it. Then it says, 'I will return to my house from which I came'; and when it comes, it finds it unoccupied, swept, and put in order. Then it goes and takes along with it seven other spirits more wicked than itself, and they go in and live there; and the last state of that man becomes worse than the first. (Matthew 12, 43-45).

Do not leave your house (heart) *"unoccupied, swept and put in order"*; rather be filled with the Holy Spirit.

We can never let down our guard. As a final instruction, remember the teaching of St. Paul in Ephesians 6:10-18. We do not go about our day without putting on our clothes. Do not go into the world with God's armor:

Finally, draw your strength from the Lord and from his mighty power. Put on the armor of God so that you may be able to stand firm against the tactics of the devil. For our struggle is not with flesh and blood but with the principalities, with the powers, with the world rulers of this present darkness, with the evil spirits in the heavens. Therefore, put on the armor of God that you may be able to resist on the evil day and, having done everything, to hold your ground. So, stand fast with your loins girded in truth, clothed with righteousness as a breastplate, and your feet shod in readiness for the gospel of peace. In all circumstances, hold faith as a shield, to quench all (the) flaming arrows of the evil one. And take the helmet of salvation and the sword of the Spirit, which is the word of God. With all prayer and supplication, pray at every opportunity in the Spirit. To that end, be watchful with all perseverance and supplication.

APENDEX 1
Steps for Self-Deliverance

The purpose of all this information is to enable you to do a self-deliverance at home for yourself. The process of self-deliverance is carried out in stages. Let's go through them one by one.

STEP ONE: Start with praise and worship. You can sing songs to praise God and to worship Him.

STEP TWO: Confess out loud Scriptures promising deliverance. Luke 10:19, Ephesians 1:7, Romans 16:20, Revelation 12:11, Colossians 2:14-15, Galatians 3:13-14, Psalms 91:3..._2 Timothy 4:18_ says And the Lord shall deliver me from every evil work, and will preserve me unto His heavenly kingdom: to whom be glory forever and ever. Amen. You should memorize _2 Tim 4:18_.

STEP THREE: Break covenants and curses to destroy their legal hold. You pray a simple prayer like this: I break any curse or covenant working against me, in the name of Jesus. (Simple prayers)

STEP FOUR: Bind all the spirits associated with those covenants and curses like this: I bind all the spirits attached or connected to the curses and covenants I have just broken, in the name of Jesus.

STEP FIVE: Lay one hand on your head and pray, Holy Ghost, cover me from the top of my head to the sole of my feet, in the name of Jesus. Begin to mention every organ of your body; kidney, liver, intestine, blood, etc. You must not rush at this level. Lay your hands-on areas that the Spirit of God leads you to.

STEP SIX: Then begin to saturate yourself with the Blood of Jesus. You do this by saying: I plead the Blood of Jesus over me. This must continue until you have a release in your spirit to stop.

STEP SEVEN: It is now, that you can demand firmly, in the name of the Lord Jesus Christ, that any spirit that is not of God should leave you. You demand it forcefully like this: In the name of the Lord Jesus Christ, I come against all you hidden spirits and I bind your activities in my life. You can no longer hide below the surface because I now recognize what you have been doing; release me, in the name of Jesus.

(If sickness is the problem, address it and say) You spirit of infirmity, I speak to you directly, get out of my life now. I am redeemed by the Blood of Jesus Christ, come out and go now. Go out with every breath by the power of the Holy Spirit. I prevail over you, in the name of Jesus.

86

STEP EIGHT: Ask for a fresh in-filling of the Holy Spirit and close the session with praises. Self-deliverance keeps you from getting sick; it removes every evil seed of the enemy; it charges your body with fire. It uproots evil plantations and builds up your confidence. Every night before you go to bed, you must remember these two important prayer points.

1. Pray for cover with the Blood of Jesus. ***Revelation 12:11*** = And they overcame him by the Blood of the Lamb, and by the word of their testimony; and they loved not their lives unto the death.
2. Pray that the Angels of God should surround you. ***Psalms 34:7*** = The Angel of the Lord encampeth round about them that fear him, and delivereth them.

No matter how sleepy you are, make sure pray these two prayer points every night. There is no reason why self-deliverance should not be effective. However, if the person seeking deliverance is under stubborn demonic control or hereditary strongman and lacks sufficient faith or authority to defeat the oppressors or living in any known sin, the evil spirits will be hard to get rid of. right.

One final word of caution. For a person to be delivered, he/she must want deliverance. Self-deliverance must not be done because of pride, shyness, the fear of possible public embarrassment, etc. Your motive for engaging in self-deliverance has to be pure.

REMEMBER: ***DELIVERANCE IS A PROCESS (((NOT A ONE-TIME EVENT)))*** AND THE LENGTH OF TIME IT TAKES DEPENDS ON SEVERAL THINGS;

1. The length of time the spirit has stayed inside a person
2. The strength and reinforcement of the spirit
3. The experience and degree of anointing upon those who are ministering the deliverance
4. The willingness of the person being delivered to be free
5. The knowledge of the Word of God and your level of hatred for sin
6. SELF-DISCIPLINE IS NECESSARY

Also, remember that bondage can be weak or strong. A weak hold can be broken quickly, whereas a stronghold may take a more time. You will not realize the strength of bondage until you faithfully and persistently work on it. You must remember that a foothold can graduate to a stronghold if left unaddressed. After this exercise, set aside some days (with fasting). DO NOT CONTINUE TO DO THE THINGS THAT CAUSED THE "it"! CHANGE YOUR HABITS TO AGREE WITH YOUR PRAYERS. AMEN.

Appendix 2

Exposing the Doors to Bondage

Part I: The bondage

1. When did this bondage start?

2. Was there any unusual things that took place (or you did) when this bondage started?

3. If this bondage started when you were a child: Do you have ancestors who have suffered from a similar kind of bondage?

4. What kind of bondage are you facing? (Fears, depression, voices in your mind, mental illness, physical illness, mental torment, spiritual torment, etc... Please be as detailed as possible.)

5. What are all the things that have impacted your life? (Parent's death, trauma, a certain situation that changed your life, anything that 'changed' you.)

Part II: Your ancestor's background

1. Do you have ancestors who have struggled with similar problems or bondages?

2. Did your bondage start as a child and appear to have no reason to be there?

3. Do you have siblings who suffer from similar bondages or oppression?

Part III: Soul ties

1. Have you been involved with extramarital sex? Are you attracted to an ex-lover? Is he or she a good/godly influence for you?

2. Have you been divorced?

3. Do you feel an unusual attraction to a past boyfriend, girlfriend or lover (who is obviously not right for you)?

4. Do you let anybody dominate, control, or make your choices you?

5. Have you ever formed a blood covenant with another person? (Blood brothers, etc.)

6. Have you ever made vows or agreements with somebody in effort to strengthen the relationship or commit yourself to each other?

7. Do you see any ungodly relationships in your past where gifts were exchanged? (Are you holding onto something that was given to you from somebody you had adultery with, etc.)

8. Have you ever had ungodly relations with any one?

9. Do you have any pictures in your possession of somebody whom you may have an ungodly soul tie with? (A picture of you with somebody you had an adultery with, etc.)

Part IV: Relationship with parents

1. What do you think of your parents?

2. How would you explain your childhood?

3. Where you close to your parents while growing up? If not, why?

4. How would you explain your relationship with your parents? Was it good, bad or very cold?

5. Did you feel rejection from your parents?

6. Was either of your parents overly passive or controlling?

7. Has either of your parents been divorced? Remarried? Are your parents divorced?

8. How would you describe your relationship with your siblings growing up?

Part V: Rejection and abuse

1. Were your parents married when you were conceived? Were you the right sex? Did your parents not want you, or want you to be different (gender, etc.) in any way? If so, explain.

2. Did you feel rejected as a child? As an adult? If so, by whom? Explain.

3. Did you face abuse? What kind (emotional, physical, sexual, etc.) and by whom?

4. Have you faced rejection from your peers, classmates, friends or those around you?

5. Have you ever been put down, belittled, or made fun of? If so, by whom? Explain.

6. If you have faced rejection or abuse, how did you respond? Do you feel you are still paying a price for it? If so, how?

7. How do you respond to rejection right now?

8. Do you reject yourself (self-rejection)? If so, why and in what ways?

Part VI: Unforgiveness or bitterness

1. Is there anybody you feel edgy around? (Don't like them, feel anything in your heart against them, etc.)

2. Do you have anything against anybody? In other words, is there anybody that you have a hard time demonstrating the love of Christ to?

3. Has anybody wronged you that you haven't forgiven from your heart (thoughts, feelings, emotions, etc.)?

4. How do your view your siblings, parents, coworkers, etc.? Do you have any hard feelings against them?

5. Do you make a habit of blaming yourself for everything? Do you obsess over your mistakes and feel unusually guilty for them?

6. Do you deeply regret things that you've done in your past? Could you kick yourself over something you've done in your past? If so, explain.

Part VII: Personality

1. Are you a very positive or negative person?

2. Do you feel confident in yourself? If so, why?

3. Do you have a low self-esteem? If so, why?

4. Are you domineering or controlling? If so, to whom, and in what ways? Why?

5. Are you an achiever? (A go-getter) If so, in what ways?

6. Do you feel that you are always right and that if everybody did everything your way, this world would be a better place to live?

7. How do you treat your children? Husband? Are you controlling, passive, etc.?

8. Do you like people to 'look at you' (as in receive attention)?

Part VIII: Emotional health

1. Do you strive to feel accepted? If so, how does this affect your lifestyle? By whom do you want to feel accepted?

2. Are you always stressed out? If so, why?

3. Do you feel hurt? If so, by whom/what and why?

4. Do you feel good about yourself? If not, why?

5. Do you feel depressed? If so, why? When did it start? Did your parents or grandparents struggle with depression? If so, then do you know when it started and why? Do you have siblings who are also struggling? Do you feel your depression is rational or irrational?

6. Do you struggle with fears? If so, what is it that you fear? (Fear of heights, dying, being hopeless, failure, never marrying, etc.)

7. Do you worry about things? What things do you worry about? Why?

8. Do you struggle with anger? Do you have a short temper?

9. Do you have any insecurity? If so, explain.

10. Do you feel any self-pity or feel sorry for yourself? Have you ever felt this? If so, why?

11. Do you find it easy to hate people? If so, over what kinds of things would a person have to do to make you hate them?

12. Do you have any irrational feelings? If so, what are they?

13. Do you feel like something is wrong with you?

14. Do you feel excessively guilty over anything? Is this a continual problem?

15. Are you very confused and forgetful? (Beyond the normal)

16. Are you aware of any emotional wounds that have affected you?

17. Have you ever been deeply embarrassed over something? What was it?

18. Have you been in or are currently experiencing very difficult (depressing) circumstances which may cause you to feel hopeless or depressed?

Part IX: Who are you in Christ? And how do you see God?

1. How do you explain your relationship with God?

2. Do you feel you aren't good enough to meet His standards?

3. Do you see Him as a loving father, or a dictator?

4. Do you believe that it's only by the Blood of Jesus that your sins are forgiven? Or do you feel you need to earn your forgiveness in any way?

5. Do you feel God's love in your life?

6. Do you feel like your sins are forgiven? Or do you feel guilty?

7. Do you feel excessively guilty in everyday life?

8. Do you feel that doing good things, you earn God's love and acceptance?

9. Do you feel that God is angry or upset with you?

Part X: Spoken curses, vows & oaths

1. Have you ever spoken something negative about yourself that has come to past? For example: "I'm sick and tired..." or "If I don't quit typing, I'm going to get arthritis!"

2. Has your parents, or those in authority over you spoken out a curse over you? For example: "You'll never amount to anything!" or "You'll never get out of debt" or "You're so dumb"

3. Have you ever made a vow out of anger? If so, what? For example: "I'll never let anybody push me around again!" or "I'm never going to be hurt again!"

4. Have you ever wished to die? Have you ever said it?

5. If you have made any vows or oaths, what are they?

Part XI: Relationships

1. Do you have many friends? What kind of people are they?

2. Do you have a hard time trying to meet new people or make friends?

3. Are you socially outgoing or shy? If so, why?

4. How would you define your relationship with your spouse?

Part XII: Sexuality

1. Have you ever had unholy sex? What kind? (Fornication, adultery, sodomy, with a child, etc.)

2. Have you struggled with lust, fantasy or unholy sexual thoughts? If so, what kind?

3. Have you been attracted to pornography?

4. Do you have homosexual thoughts and desires? If so, have you acted upon those feelings?

5. How do you feel about your sexuality? (Do you feel dirty about it, or do you feel it's a wonderful blessing that God's given you?)

6. Do you withhold sex from your spouse or are you fidgety? Do you enjoy a healthy relationship with your spouse sexually? How does he or she react?

7. Have you ever been raped or sexually abused?

8. Have you ever woke up and felt a sexual presence with you? There are demons that imitate male and female functions, and stimulate their host (a person) sexually (beyond the normal 'wet dream').

9. Do you struggle or have you struggled with masturbation?

10. Do you struggle or have you struggled with any other sexual related thoughts, desires, or bondages?

11. Is there anything sexually that you are ashamed of?

Part XIII: Addictions

1. Do you have any addictions? If so, what kind? (Drugs, alcohol, smoking, eating, sex, TV, etc.) When did they start?

2. Did anybody else in your family (siblings, ancestors, etc.) have a struggle with any addictions? If so, what? Who?

3. Have you ever had, or currently have any sort of obsession over anything? If so, what?

Part XIV: False religions

Examples of false religions: Buddhism, Hindu, Jehovah Witness, Mormonism, Christian Scientists, eastern religions, etc.

1. Have you ever been involved with any false religions? If so, why, when and how long? How do you feel about those beliefs now?

2. Have you ever been involved in any secret societies such as Freemasonry? If so, how deep were you involved?

Part XV: The occult

1. Have you ever shown interest in the occult? If so, in what ways? (Read up on it, dabbled in it, etc.)

2. Do you still feel drawn or attracted to the occult?

3. Have you had any interest in horror or thriller style movies or novels? Are you still attracted to these things?

4. Have you ever made a vow with the devil? If so, what?

5. Married Satan?

6. Worshipped a demon or Satan?

7. Have you ever put a curse or spell on somebody?

8. Are you aware of any curses or spells placed on you? If so, what? Who did it?

9. Dabbled with an Ouija board? If so, why?

10. Ever been a member of a coven (group of 13 witches)? Explain.

11. Communicated with the dead? Explain.

12. Told somebody's fortune or went to see a fortune teller? Explain.

13. Ever read your horoscope?

14. Watched or been involved in a séance? Explain.

15. Have you been involved or a victim of Satanic Ritual Abuse (SRA)? Explain.

16. Been baptized into a false religion or any other evil baptism? If so, what were you baptized into? When?

17. Have you ever had a spirit guide?

18. Have you ever been involved with meditation, yoga, karate, or related activities?

19. Were you or anybody in your family superstitious? If so, who?

20. Ever been involved in astral travel? (Out of body)

21. If you have made any vows or oaths, what are they? Were there any sacrifices or rituals that were accompanied with them?

22. Have you ever made a blood pact before? If so, with whom (including persons, demons and Satan) and for what purpose?

23. Have you ever partaken in automatic writing, automatic drawing or automatic painting?

24. Have you ever been involved in Yoga, transcendental meditation, or similar activities?

25. Have you ever sought healing from a spiritual source other than Jesus Christ? (New age healing, energy healing, etc.)

26. Any other involvement in the occult? Explain.

Part XVI: Un-confessed sins

1. Are there any un-confessed sins that you have not repented of? (Usually something you've done, that you know is wrong, but won't admit to it. An abortion, stealing, etc. are some examples.)

2. Is there anything you've been hiding inside that you haven't confessed?

3. Do you feel excessively guilty over something(s) you've done in the past? If so, what?

Part XVII: Cursed objects

1. Do you have any idols, occult rings, or anything that could hold evil spiritual value in your home? If so, what? Any objects that hold evil spiritual value must be destroyed.

2. Do you have any gifts saved from sinful relationships? If so, explain. For example, if a man gives a woman a personal gift during an adultery that needs to be sold or destroyed.

Part XVIII: Severe trauma, abuse & disassociation

1. Have you ever been exposed to extreme abuse or a traumatic experience? Did it have a drastic effect on your emotional or mental system? If so, what happen? How did it affect you?

2. Have you ever disassociated or been diagnosed with Dissociative Identity Disorder (DID) or Multiple Personality Disorder (MPD)?

3. Are you aware of any alters (other personalities) that you may have? (If so, tell me about them)

4. Do you have a memory gap where you cannot remember a certain time of your life?

5. Do you have false memories of things that really didn't take place?

6. Have you ever been in a car accident or other traumatic situation? Have you ever witnessed a tragedy in real life?

Part XIX: Weaknesses

1. Do you struggle with any habitual sins? If so, what? Do you want to break those bad habits?

2. Do you struggle with any weaknesses such as lust, anger, hate, etc.? If so, what? Do you know where they came from or how they got started? Do you want to break free from those weaknesses?

Part XX: Pregnancy issues

1. Have you ever said something along the lines of, "I will never have children"?

2. Have you ever had an abortion or attempted one?

3. Have you ever had incest or ungodly sexual relations with somebody related to you? (See Leviticus 20:19-21, as this can cause a curse to land upon you which needs to be broken)

Part XXI: Other things to look for

1. Have you ever tried drugs? If so, how much, and how did it affect you? Why did you try drugs?

2. Have you ever thought about or attempted suicide?

3. Do you have any physical or mental disabilities, diseases or illnesses? Explain.

4. Do you want, and are willing to be delivered? Are you willing to give up those demon spirits and maybe make some lifestyle changes in order to keep your deliverance?

5. Do you experience unusual confusion settle upon you as you try to pray and read the Bible?

6. What kind of music do you like? (Please list all styles of music you currently enjoy, and give examples in each category you list, such as some names of artists and songs)

7. Have you previously enjoyed hard rock, metal, acid, alternative, rap, new age, or any other kind of worldly music? (Please provide some examples of artists and songs from each genre (type/style) of music you list)

8. Have you had any nightmares or weird experiences at night while supposedly sleeping?

9. Have you ever been in a trance or had an out of body experience?

10. Have you ever noticed time slipped right out from under you? For example, you look at your watch and its 7:00pm, then you look again what seemed like 15 minutes later and its 2:00am. This is a sign of a trance.

11. Have you ever touched or kissed a dead body? If so, explain whom and why and what happened afterwards.

12. Do you feel that you somehow have to earn your forgiveness? Do you 'wonder' if your sins are truly forgiven -- all of them? Are you aware of any signs of legalism or religious spirits operating in your mind?

13. Do you have any physical infirmities, sickness or diseases? If so, please list them.

14. Are you on any medications? If so, please explain.

15. Are you entertained by movies or TV shows which glorify death, murder, pain or suffering of others? Please explain.

16. Have you ever had any other kind of weird encounter with the spiritual realm?

Use this information to expose the root cause of the "it".

REFERENCES

1. Gary R. Collins, *Christian Counseling: A Comprehensive Guide*, 3rd Addition, Revised and Updated, NavPress, Colorado Springs, Colorado. ISBN 1418503290

2. Beilby, J.K. & P.R. Eddy. *Understanding Spiritual Warfare: Four Views*. Grand Rapids, Michigan: Baker, 2012.

3. Boyd, G.A., *God at War: The Bible and Spiritual Conflict*. Downers Grove, Illinois: IVP, 1997.

4. Hiebert, P. "Spiritual Warfare and Worldview"

5. Stedman, R.C, *Spiritual Warfare: Winning the Daily Battle with Satan.* Portland, Oregon: Multnomah, 1975.

6. Pirolo, N., *Prepare for Battle: Basic Training in Spiritual Warfare*, San Diego, California: Emmaus Road, International, 1997.

7. Arnold, E. C., *3 Crucial Questions about Spiritual Warfare*, Grand Rapids, Michigan: Baker, 1997.1

8. Rita Bennett, You Can Be Emotionally Free, 1982 ISBN 978 0 88270 748 8

9. Rita Bennett, Emotionally Free, 1982, ISBN 0 86065 194 0
   Publishers, PO Box 777,

10. Tonbridge, Kent TN 11 0ZS, England, 1997, reprinted 2004). ISBN 1-85240-110-9. (Available in the US through the Arsenal Bookstore, 11005 Voyager Parkway, Colorado Springs, CO 80921.)

11. John and Paula Sandford, Healing the Wounded Spirit (Victory House, 1985). ISBN 0-932081-14-2.

12. Norma Dearing, The Healing Touch (Chosen Books, 2002). ISBN 0-8007-9302-1. Charles Kraft, Deep Wounds, Deep Healing (Servant Pub., 1993). ISBN 0-89283-784-5.

13. Derek Prince, God's Remedy for Rejection (Whitaker House, 1993). ISBN 088368-864-6.

14. Francis and Judith MacNutt, Praying for Your Unborn Child (1989). ISBN 0-38523-2829. (Available from www.Christianhealingmin.org, 904-765-3332.)

15. Thomas Verney, MD, The Secret Life of the Unborn Child (Summit Books, 1981).

16. Anderson, Winning Spiritual Warfare 1990 ISBN 13: 978-0-89081-868-8 James

17. Friesen, Uncovering the Mystery of MPD, 1997 ISBN 1-56819-062-7

18. Diane Hawkins, Multiple Identities, 2009 ISBN 978-0-9708073-6-6,

19. Restoration in Christ Ministries, http://www.rcm-usa.org/index.htm

20. Francis MacNutt, Deliverance from Evil Spirits, 1995, 0-8007-9232-7, Chap 17, pp 223-235 (best introductory material)

21. Daniel Ryder, Breaking the Circle of SRA, 1992, 0-89638-258-3 (an excellent book by a Christian counselor)

22. Margaret Smith, Ritual Abuse, what it is, why it happens, how to help, 1993, 0-06-250214-X (in depth information about SRA and MPD)

23. The Christian Bible

24. The following associations focus on trauma and disassociation www.sidran.org, www.issd.org

25. Pentecost, J.D., *Your Adversary the Devil.* Grand Rapids, Michigan: Zondervan, 1969

About the Author
Dr. Paulette Douglas

Dr. Paulette Douglas truly epitomizes elegance in living a saved, sanctified and Holy life, set apart from the secular world! Dr. Douglas is an ordained minister with the Pentecostal Assemblies of the World, an anointed national and international Evangelist, teacher and preacher. Dr. Paulette Douglas is renowned for the ministry of exhortation to the Body of Christ through deliverance, inner healing, salvation and biblical counseling at seminars, prayer clinics, crusades and conferences. She has established three churches and assisted in establishing many other churches, ministries and colleges as she serves on the Body of Christ for Jesus. Dr. Douglas was baptized in the name of Jesus Christ and filled with the Holy Ghost in 1977. She was called to the ministry in 1981, taught bible study at Pacific Bell for nine years which established the Radiant Life in Christ Ministries. She was the founder and pastor of the Radiant Life in Christ Community Church in Baldwin Park, California for nearly four years. Dr. Douglas retired in 1996 with full benefits from AT&T after 26 years of service. God introduced Dr. Douglas to the LOVE and HERO of her life, Bishop Robert T. Douglas Sr. They were married, the ministries merged, and she became the First Lady of the Jacob's Ladder Family, the Women's Ministry Director, the Church Executive Administrator and the Dean of the California University of Theology. Dr. Robert and Paulette Douglas are the proud parents of three wonderful children, Shakinah, Robert Jr. and Sondra Imani. They are also blessed with two granddaughters, Demi and Rob'Ann (butter ball) four grandsons, Dylan, Dominick Terrell, the twins Canden and Caden. Seven Godchildren and twelve God -grandchildren. Dr. Douglas is a graduate from Fuller Theological Seminary, Pasadena, California, Pentecostal Bible College, Ministerial Training Institute of Inglewood, California and Aenon Bible College West Coast. She has a Bachelors degree in Biblical Studies, a Masters degree in Theology, a PhD in Theology, Administration and a PhD in Biblical Counseling. She has earned certificates from California Christian Leadership of Orange County in biblical counseling, Zoe Christian Leadership Training Institute, Church Growth International, Seoul Korea and School of World Missions and Evangelism, Los Angeles. Dr. Douglas is formerly the Dean/Professor of the Inglewood Ministerial Training Institute of Inglewood, the Inland Empire Ministerial Training Institute, the Tri-County Ministerial Training Institute (San Bernardino, Riverside and Los Angeles counties) and the Living Waters Bible College, Rialto California. Dr. Douglas is presently the Dean of Colleges and Professor for the California District Council Aenon Bible College and Institutes, the Jacob's Ladder California University of Theology and Aenon Bible Institute CDC Extension Campus in Inglewood, California and the American College Theological Seminary International University (ACTS). All schools are fully accredited institutions for pastors, evangelist, teachers and anyone who has the call of God on their lives for ministry. Dr. Douglas is currently the CDC International Missions President and the past Church/Extension/Evangelism/Altar Director for the California District Council of the Pentecostal Assemblies of the World, Inc. Past Evangelism President for the CHDC Area 2 and has worked with the PAW Evangelism Ministry for more than 35 years. Dr. Paulette Douglas is the published author of the book series "Get Rid of It before It Gets Rid of You". Self-Help Instructions on how to correct and receive deliverance in every area of your life. Dr. Douglas portrays tremendous strength and endurance in the Lord by jointly sharing the vision and love for God with Bishop Douglas. Her primary objective in life is to be that "Excellent Woman of God, walking in His Divine favor.

**Books and Recourses Compiled by
Dr. Paulette Douglas**

"How to Get Rid of "it", Before "it" Gets Rid of You" Series (12 Books on Self Deliverance)

Volume One- Healing and Deliverance from Additions

Volume Two- Healing and Deliverance from Sexual Additions

Volume Three- Healing and Deliverance from Personality Disorders

Volume Four- Healing and Deliverance from Negative Relationships

Volume Five- Healing and Deliverance Through Spiritual Warfare

Volume Six- Healing and Deliverance from Negatives Attitudes

Volume Seven- Healing and Deliverance from Success Hindrances

Volume Eight- Healing and Deliverance from Tormenting Emotions

Volume Nine- Healing and Deliverance from Spiritual Weakness

Volume Ten- Healing and Deliverance from Salvation Issues

Volume Eleven- Healing and Deliverance from Domestic Problems

Volume Twelve- Healing and Deliverance Through Biblical Counseling

How to Have an Anointed Altar Workers Ministry

How to Have an Effective Prayer and Fasting Life

How to Walk in Your Grace as the Wife of a Minister, Deacon, Pastor, or Bishop

How to be an Effective Life Coach